November [...]
Dear L[...]
to the s[...]
and exciting[...] would be
Thought this [...] place for us to start.
#sidehustle
xx
Tina

LET'S TALK PODCASTING

AMANDA CUPIDO

LET'S TALK PODCASTING

THE ESSENTIAL GUIDE TO DOING IT RIGHT

PPS PUB

PPS PUB

326 Adelaide Street W, 6th Floor,
Toronto, ON M5V 1R3

This book is presented solely for educational purposes. Although the author and publisher have made every effort to ensure that the information in this book was correct at press time, the author and publisher do not assume and hereby disclaim any liability to any party for any loss, damage, or disruption caused by errors or omissions, whether such errors or omissions result from negligence, accident, or any other cause.

Let's Talk Podcasting: The Essential Guide To Doing It Right
Copyright © 2018 by Amanda Cupido
All rights reserved
Printed in Canada

No part of this book may be used or reproduced in any manner whatsoever without written permission except in the case of brief quotations embodied in critical articles and reviews. For more information or to write to the publiher, please address your mail to the address above. PPS Publishing books may be purchased for educational, business, or sales promotional use. For information, please email the Special Markets Department at SPsales@ ppspublishing.com.

Library and Archives Canada Cataloguing in Publication

Cupido, Amanda, author
Let's talk podcasting : the essential guide to doing it
right / Amanda Cupido.

Issued in print and electronic formats.
ISBN 978-1-988994-06-2 (softcover).--ISBN 978-1-988994-07-9
(HTML)

1. Podcasting. I. Title.

TK5105.887.C87 2018   006.7'876   C2018-904603-1
                                            C2018-904604-X

Designed by Leah Concepcion-Vanderbyl
ISBN (print): 978-1-988994-06-2 | (ePub): 978-1-988994-07-9

Icons provided by Vecteezy.com

PRAISE FOR *LET'S TALK PODCASTING*

"Amanda's approach to storytelling and podcast production is passionate and clear and that comes across in spades in *Let's Talk Podcasting*. [...] She speaks to you at eye-level and if you have any inkling to create a podcast yourself, you'll be glad you have her voice in your head and this book in your hand."

—**PAULA BRANCATI**, *Producer/Actor, Co-Owner of BrancSeater Productions Inc.*

"Like great radio, a great podcast episode should keep you on the edge of your seat, lost in the conversation; unable to turn it off. Not everyone understands the art of great storytelling, but Amanda Cupido does. *Let's Talk Podcasting* is a must read for anyone who wants to keep you at their podcast party."

—**KYM GEDDES**, *News Director, NEWSTALK 1010 CFRB*

"[...] Along with tips and tricks to mastering the process, I loved the section on how Amanda did it all herself, with personal advice and helpful anecdotes tied to her critical and commercial success in this space. Affordable and portable, I highly recommended Amanda Cupido's *Let's Talk Podcasting*."

—**MARC SALTZMAN**, *Host & Producer of the Tech it Out podcast*

PRAISE FOR *LET'S TALK PODCASTING*

"From choosing a format to selecting equipment, creating a script, and promoting your show, Amanda gives you the info you need to get on the air. She brings the same expertise and energy to this book as she does to her classes. You, too, can create a successful podcast!"

—**BETH AGNEW**, *Chair, School of Media, Seneca College*

"Podcasting is a phenomenal way to target and engage an audience. [Cupido] outlines how to produce content —explore ideas, tell stories and conduct interviews— that can entertain and engage your listeners. Whether you want to promote a brand, launch a business or pursue your passion, the book offers everything you need to know about buying equipment and designing your studio, even if it's from home."

—**JANICE NEIL**, *Chair, School of Journalism, Ryerson University*

ABOUT THE AUTHOR

AMANDA CUPIDO is an award-winning podcast producer and instructor at Seneca College's School of Media. Previously, she worked as a major market radio producer, reporter and news anchor. Amanda has a Bachelor of Journalism from Ryerson University and is in the midst of completing her Master of Professional Studies in Psychology of Leadership at Pennsylvania State University.

For every person that has taken the time to be interviewed for a podcast I was working on. Thank you for trusting me with your story.

And for every person who I've subjected to listening to my many draft podcast episodes before sharing them with the world. Your patience, feedback and encouragement is what has kept me going.

ACKNOWLEDGMENTS

Newstalk 1010 CFRB — the first radio station that invested in me as an audio storyteller and helped me develop my voice and confidence on air.

MediaFace — the digital content agency that supported my research in the podcast space and fueled my first production of an award-winning podcast series.

Beth Agnew	**Teina Petropoulos**
Chris Boyce	**Steve Pratt**
Paula Brancati	**Nick Quah**
Barb Caines	**Ryerson School of Journalism**
Doris Chung	**Anna Sale**
Amanda De Souza	**Marc Saltzman**
Drew Garner	**Seneca School of Media**
Kym Geddes	**Shopify**
Jacky Habib	**Soho House Toronto**
Pamela Johnston	**Leah Concepcion-Vanderbyl**
Lumbrick	**Sarah Vermunt**
Omar Murji	**Anne-Marie Vettorel**
Janice Neil	**Vista Radio**
Pacific Content	**Werk It Podcast Conference**
Neil Parmar	**World Vision**

Thank you.

FOREWORD
by Chris Boyce

When I began my career in radio thirty years ago, your ability to talk to an audience was completely dependent on whether you controlled the means of distribution. To broadcast you needed a frequency and to get a frequency you needed a licence. And those licences were a scarce commodity. There were only so many available in each local market, so each licence was incredibly valuable. The gatekeepers who had the licences to broadcast controlled what the audience listened to. And the value of the licence combined with the cost of the gear that you needed to make great sounding radio ensured the whole thing remained a big ticket professional enterprise.

As a bright-eyed university student graduating in 1994 from the Radio & Television program at Ryerson University, it was inconceivable to me that one day I'd be able to create my own audio programming, in my living room and distribute it to a worldwide audience. In those days editing audio still meant physically cutting tape with razor blade! But in the span of ten short years, audio production went from something that took place in giant studios filled with high end gear costing hundreds of thousands of dollars to something you could do in your basement on your laptop. And when Apple added podcasts to iTunes in June 2005, you no longer needed that broadcast licence to get your programming in front of an audience.

In a few short years creating audio programming and distributing it worldwide went from being something that a few select people could do to something anyone could do. And although it took another decade for podcasting to really take off, its rise was a seismic shift, a democratization of the means of distribution.

But just because anyone has the ability to create a podcast and share it with a worldwide audience, doesn't mean they're able to create a compelling listening experience. Today, Apple Podcasts features more than half a million different podcasts. But the reality is that only a tiny sliver of that number contribute to the bulk of the listening. The rest are heard by a handful of people. Because the reality is that while technology enables anyone to make a podcast, it's a hell of a lot of work to create one that's compelling to listen to. The barrier to entry today is creativity and skill, not money and scarce access to the airwaves.

Over my career I've been lucky. I've got to help create and launch countless new shows and work with some of the best audio storytellers in the business. When I ran CBC Radio (Canada's public broadcaster) I got to program two national radio networks full of some of the best programming in the world. But I think the past few years working in podcasting has been the most creatively rewarding work that I've done. And I finally get to reach that worldwide audience, working from my living room, in my pajamas if I want.

If you're wondering what podcasting is all about, this book is a guide to all the basics that you need to get started. From deconstructing different show formats to recommendations on what gear to use, Amanda Cupido even shares a case study on how she took everything she learned to make a podcast for World Vision Canada.

The beauty of podcasting is that anyone can do it. Podcasts from kids in their basement sit alongside big budget productions from Hollywood celebrities. Today what it takes to be successful is creativity and skill. So get out there and start creating.

— **Chris Boyce**
Co-owner & Principal, Pacific Content

CONTENTS

XIII   *Foreword*
XXI   *Introduction*

PART 1: THE FOUNDATION

29   **The Evolution of Podcasting**
33   **Who's Listening?**
39   **Ads in Podcasting**

PART 2: WHAT'S OUT THERE?

47   **Overall Stats from Current Podcasts**
49   **Formats, Genres & What's Missing**
55   **Lessons from Notable Podcasts**
65   **Ad Styles & Best Practices**

PART 3: WHAT'S NEXT?

73	The Rise of the Podcast Celebrity
77	The Future of Branded Podcasts
81	Podcasts Going to Live Audiences
83	Podcast Awards
85	Who to Keep an Eye On

PART 4: DOING IT YOURSELF

93	Starting Your Own Podcast
99	Production Equipment
105	Recording Techniques
109	Scripting 101
115	Post Production
123	Promotion Strategy
127	Audience Engagement
129	Hiring Support for Your Podcast

PART 5: HOW I DID IT

137	Behind the Scenes: *A Pitch for Change*
143	Behind the Scenes: *New Lens Travel*
157	Conclusion
161	*Glossary*

> "*Great stories happen to those who can tell them.*"
>
> —IRA GLASS

INTRODUCTION

There's something magical about using sounds to paint a picture in people's minds. Just like the intimacy of radio, when audio storytelling is done right, people are transported. They feel connected to the voice speaking to them and invested in the story being told. Sounds can paint any picture, create any landscape and jump from one location to another with seamless transitions. Audio storytelling is a true art and sharing this type of art is now easier than ever.

Back in 2005, the editors of the New Oxford American Dictionary chose "podcast" as the Word of the Year. Just over a decade later, podcasts are increasingly popular and have even been referred to as the "new blogging."

According to Apple, there are more than 1 billion people who have subscribed to a podcast and many find themselves wanting to create their own. The reason? Well it varies: from simply wanting to entertain, to raising awareness about an issue, or even as a method of building a brand.

Social media platforms are adapting to accommodate this love for broadcasting audio, too. In early 2018, it was reported that Facebook was testing voice clip status updates as a form of "micropodcasting."

This, combined with the increase of cars that have wifi capabilities, means that podcasts are going to be more accessible than ever. It's not shocking to hear that audiences are now choosing to stream a podcast when they would typically be listening to the radio — it's a natural progression for podcasts to become a more prominent companion while on the road.

These are just a few examples of how audio storytelling is one of the most versatile ways of reaching audiences where they're at. If it's not in the car, it's through headphones on the train, while on a run or even while falling asleep. In a culture where the most valuable thing is time, podcasting allows people to be entertained, work on their professional development or catch up on the news in a simple, efficient way.

WHY READ THIS BOOK?

This book is meant for people who are interested in starting their own podcast, want to invest in a podcast for their business, or are just genuinely interested in familiarizing themselves with the podcast landscape right now and what's to come.

This book is made up of five sections:

PART 1: THE FOUNDATION

This includes the history of podcasting, current listenership and how advertisers are taking advantage of the medium.

PART 2: WHAT'S OUT THERE?

Here we'll look at the different genres/formats of podcasts and highlight some best practices using current podcasts as examples. We'll also look at how to create podcast ads.

PART 3: WHAT'S NEXT?

This section will explore how the medium is projected to expand, and who to keep an eye on.

PART 4: DOING IT YOURSELF

This is where you'll find all the nitty gritty details of starting a podcast. I'll outline what equipment you'll need, how to upload, and important tips to keep in mind when recording.

PART 5: HOW I DID IT

This is where I pull back the curtain and show you how I created some of my recent projects. This behind the scenes section will give you an idea of what it looks like when you put everything you've learned in this book into practice!

WHY SHOULD YOU TRUST ME?

Totally fair question. Here's where I'm coming from...

My background is in radio. I worked in both AM and FM settings and spent time in several different roles around the station; I worked as a member of the promotions team, then as a producer, reporter, news anchor and morning show co-host. Most of my time was spent in major market radio in Toronto, Ontario. This is where my love for audio began.

During this time, "podcasting" started to get its initial buzz and I began getting requests to produce them. My first client was a thought leader who wanted to embrace the new medium. I created my first series. Given my skill set, I was able to do end-to-end production and realized... *damn, I love this*.

My career then took a shift and I started working full time with a digital content agency producing branded video content. As the podcast scene evolved, I kept a close eye on the latest listenership research and what kind of content was excelling. I made my case for why the content agency should start offering podcasts to clients and was given the green light to build that part of the business. We sourced the necessary equipment and I led a team that pitched, produced and sold podcasts.

Fast forward to present day. I'm now working as a freelance podcast producer and as an instructor at Seneca College's School of Media. Naturally, my classes are focused on audio storytelling, where I get to encourage students to experiment with this art (shoutout to any of my students reading this!) and hopefully love it as much as I do.

Are we good? Hope so. Because here we go...

Part 1

THE FOUNDATION

Chapter 1

THE EVOLUTION OF PODCASTING

First, let's get this out of the way: a podcast is a downloadable audio file that is a form of on-demand radio. Platforms that host these files typically allow listeners to also "subscribe," which means that your device will automatically be updated with the latest episodes that are released. If someone does not have a device they want these files downloaded to, podcasts can also be streamed straight from their host site.

Podcasts vary in length, subject matter and format. In this book we will take a deeper look at some of these aspects and how they resonate with the listener.

If you're curious about the origin of the word itself, look to Apple. It began as a combination of the words "iPod" and "broadcast". Podcasts are now available on more than just Apple devices, but iTunes is still seen as the leading platform for the medium. Many will also turn to Apple's "top downloads" list to determine which podcasts are the most popular.

As Canadian podcast producer Steve Pratt said, "podcasts are to radio what Netflix is to TV." People love Netflix for delivering niche, quality content in mass amounts. Just as people binge-watch TV shows, the hunger is equally (if not, more) prominent for audio entertainment.

SO HOW DID WE GET TO WHERE WE ARE NOW?

It all began with what Pratt calls the "first wave" in 2004 to 2005. This was when the term podcasting started picking up steam and people were experimenting with the new medium by uploading a lot of unedited conversations. It was a fairly easy and inexpensive way for people to broadcast online. To this day, many people still continue to publish in this fashion, but without a strategy, they're usually short-lived or have a hard time growing their audience. We will take a closer look at this type of content and correlating stats in Chapter 4.

The second wave began in 2014, which was sparked by Serial: a podcast hosted by investigative American journalist Sarah Koenig. Week by week she released episodes telling the true story of the death of a high school student in 1999, whose convicted murderer is still claiming he's innocent. She interviews him, people in the community and other notable characters from the case. It ends with no real conclusion and leaves the listener with the question: did he do it?

Not only did it win a Peabody Award in 2015 for its innovative long-format storytelling, but it was deemed a "new genre of storytelling" and "podcasting's first breakout hit." Apple also reported it was the fastest podcast to reach 5 million downloads and streams.

Hence, the coined phrase "The Serial Effect". Following Serial, several podcasts were produced in the same format with the same quality of production. Businesses were launched, audiences grew and advertisers were interested.

DID YOU KNOW?

If you're curious about the origin of the word "podcast", look to Apple. First used in 2004, it began as a combination of the words "iPod" and "broadcast".

Chapter 2

WHO'S LISTENING?

Knowing who's listening is important whether you're looking to start your own podcast (since you have to start thinking about who you'll want to target!) or want to invest in advertising on a podcast (are these audiences who you're trying to reach?), so bear with me here.

Edison Research is known for digging into the podcast listening habits of Americans. According to their 2016 report, "podcast listening showed sharp gains on both a monthly basis (17% to 21%) and weekly (10% to 13%)." The audience is also considered affluent, with 41% coming from a household with incomes of at least $75K. In addition, they're highly educated, with most of them having some grad schooling or advanced degrees.

ESTIMATED 112 MILLION

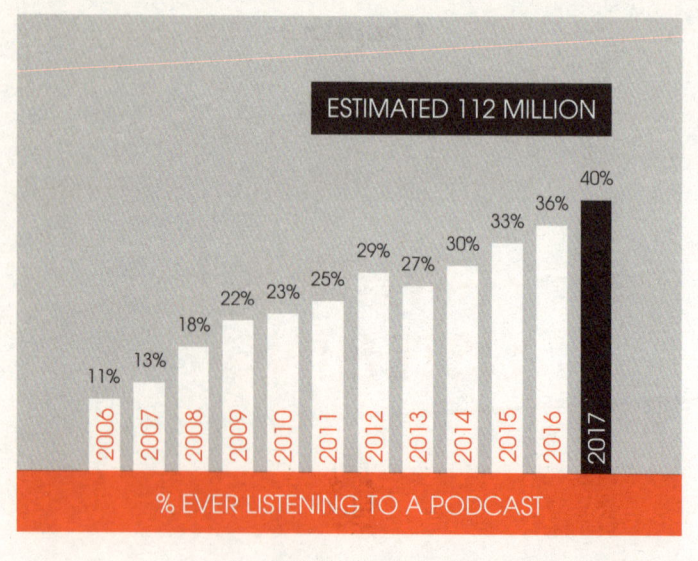

Year	%
2006	11%
2007	13%
2008	18%
2009	22%
2010	23%
2011	25%
2012	29%
2013	27%
2014	30%
2015	33%
2016	36%
2017	40%

% EVER LISTENING TO A PODCAST

ABOVE *statistics from Edison Research.*

In their 2017 report, the foundation of who listens has stayed relatively the same, but the number of listeners continues to grow. Monthly podcast listeners went from 21% to 24% and overall listenership went up as well.

These numbers are also predicted to continue to skyrocket according to Activate Analysis, Bridge Ratings and Edison Research.

Of American podcast listeners, an estimated 42 million of them listen on a weekly basis, with an average of five podcasts per week. The audience also skews slightly more male with 56% (see figure on page 34).

A majority are listening from home with listening in cars coming in second. As cars begin to increasingly offer wifi capabilities, I suspect this percentage will shift.

Podcast listeners are more likely to follow brands on social media. Those who listen to podcasts, listen to them more than they listen to the radio.

They're loyal listeners and, according to Midroll, 61% report buying something they heard about from a podcast ad.

In Canada, the stats are similar. According to a 2017 report conducted by the Globe and Mail, Ulster Media and Audience Insights, nearly 10 million Canadian adults have listened to podcasts in the past year. That's 34 percent of the 18+ population. Most listen on a weekly basis and the gender split sways slightly more male. In line with the Edison research, Canadian listeners also tend to be highly educated and affluent.

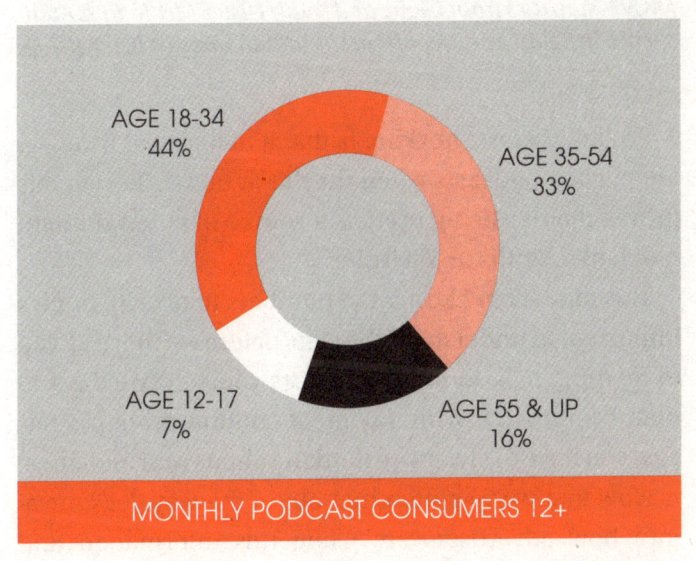

AGE 18-34 44%
AGE 35-54 33%
AGE 12-17 7%
AGE 55 & UP 16%

MONTHLY PODCAST CONSUMERS 12+

ABOVE *statistics from Triton Digital.*

% WHO LISTEN IN EACH LOCATION

- 87%
- 55%
- 36%
- 22%

AVERAGE % OF TIME IN EACH LOCATION

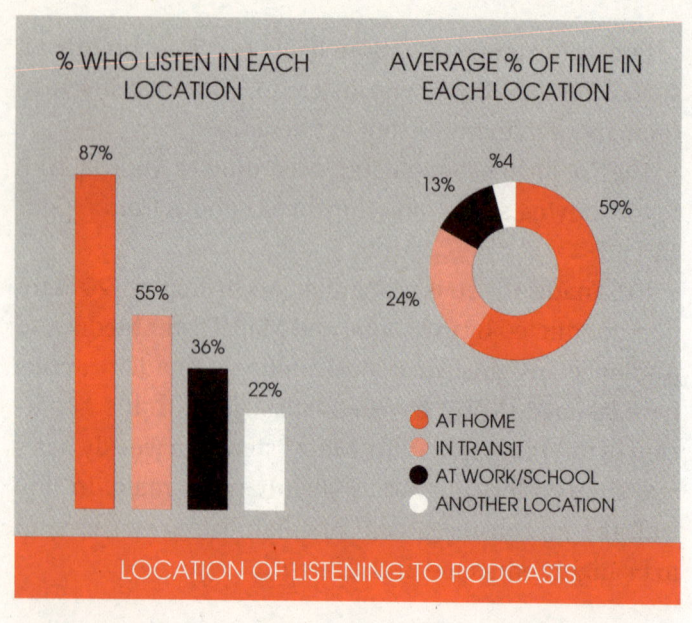

- 59%
- 24%
- 13%
- %4

● AT HOME
● IN TRANSIT
● AT WORK/SCHOOL
○ ANOTHER LOCATION

LOCATION OF LISTENING TO PODCASTS

ABOVE *statistics from Globe and Mail, Ulster Media and Audience Insights' 2017 report on Canadian podcast listenership.*

Probably most shocking is that a majority of listeners are playing podcasts when they're at home. To me, this proves that it's being used as a source of entertainment much like Netflix or YouTube.

This may seem like a lot of numbers to take in, but it's important to understand the stats before we move ahead to learning how to make podcasts yourself (we'll get to that, I promise!). With any great communication strategy, you have to always be thinking about your audience.

Now that we've gotten that out of the way, let's move into how advertisers are using this information and where the appetite is for marketers.

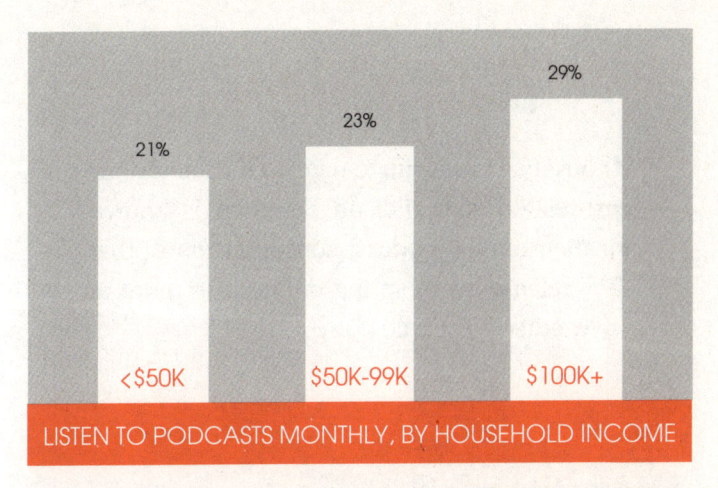

Chart: Listen to podcasts monthly, by household income
- <$50K: 21%
- $50K–99K: 23%
- $100K+: 29%

LISTEN TO PODCASTS MONTHLY, BY HOUSEHOLD INCOME

ABOVE *statistics from Globe and Mail, Ulster Media and Audience Insights' 2017 report on Canadian podcast listenership.*

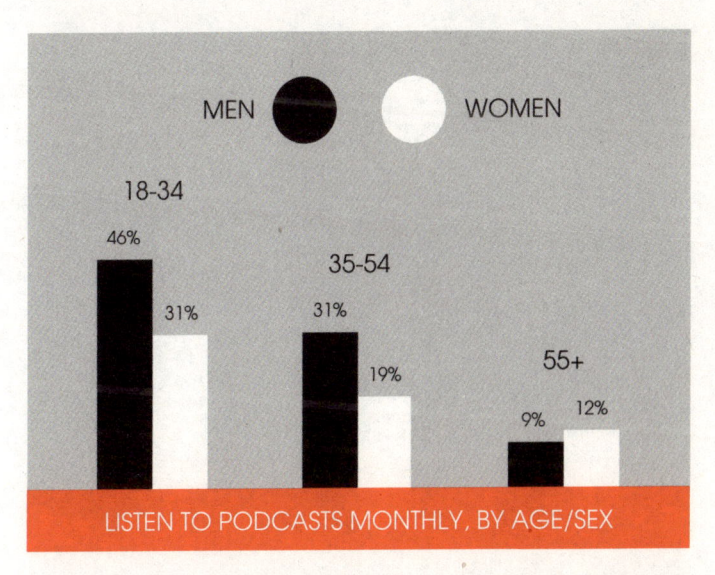

Chart: Listen to podcasts monthly, by age/sex

MEN ● WOMEN ○

- 18–34: Men 46%, Women 31%
- 35–54: Men 31%, Women 19%
- 55+: Men 9%, Women 12%

LISTEN TO PODCASTS MONTHLY, BY AGE/SEX

ABOVE *statistics from Globe and Mail, Ulster Media and Audience Insights' 2017 report on Canadian podcast listenership.*

🔍 DID YOU KNOW?

If you'd like to stay up to date on the latest podcast-related stats, Edison Research is known for their annual podcast consumer report that they release every spring online. See more at www.edisonresearch.com.

Chapter 3

ADS IN PODCASTING

I'm going to tackle this topic from several angles. First, let's talk to the people who are thinking about placing ads in a podcast. This information is also useful if you're trying to pitch a marketing department to set aside a budget to invest in podcast ads.

So, why are podcast ads effective? Research by AdWeek shows that people prefer ads in podcasts over any other digital medium and that 45 percent of listeners say they're "likely to visit an advertiser's website after hearing an audio promo."

It shouldn't be that shocking. Audiences tend to develop personal connections with hosts on audio platforms. When they're listening to someone as part of their daily routine, especially in intimate environments like in the car, they build a relationship with them. Having a host vouch for a product or brand resonates with people in a different way than traditional ads, which explains why so many are likely to visit the advertiser's website after hearing it.

Anecdotally, I know that the producer of the podcast WTF with Marc Maron has said that they have especially loyal audiences. Through doing their own surveying, they found that 80 percent of his listeners have gone and bought products that Marc has mentioned on the show.

Now, it's important to note that it takes time to build this sort of trust with your listenership. Advertisers are also looking for specific numbers of downloads before investing.

With that, let's break it down for those of you wanting to sell your own ads.

HOW MUCH MONEY CAN I MAKE FROM ADS?

Typically, advertisers are looking to be paired with podcasts that get at least 20,000 downloads per episode. 15-second ads at the beginning of a podcast typically cost around $18 per 1000 CPM (cost per thousand listens). For 60 seconds in the middle of a podcast, the price is around $25 per 1000 CPM.

This might sound pricey compared to radio ads, but advertisers are willing to pay since audiences are more niche and less likely to skip. When commercials play on the radio, people are known to hit the next preset station.

Comparatively, when people are listening to a podcast, there are no other ones queued up that they're flipping to. They're in it for the long haul. A more captive audience? It's an advertiser's dream.

> ## QUICK TIP
>
> For ease of math purposes, let's say your podcast averages 10,000 listens per episode.
>
> 18 x 10 (for the 10,000 listens) = **$180** is the cost to the sponsor for a pre-roll.
>
> 25 x 10 (for the 10,000 listens) = **$250** is the cost to the sponsor for a Mid-Roll.
>
> Therefore, your 10,000 per episode podcast would cost a sponsor **$430** for a pre-Roll/Mid-Roll Combo.
>
> Let's say you allow 2 sponsors per episode, now you're making **$860** per episode.

HOW ARE ADVERTISERS GETTING PAIRED WITH PODCASTS?

Sometimes individual companies are striking deals with individual podcasts, but most of the time, the deal is done on a larger scale.

There are several podcast networks that empower podcasters to create shows while the sales and marketing is left to a team that works for the network. One example of a network is Radiotopia, which has about 17 different podcasts. The network works with advertisers to match them with shows, taking into consideration the content and audience of their roster of podcasts and the product/service that is being promoted.

So, yes, there are people listening and, yes, there's money to be made. But it's important to realize that it doesn't happen overnight. Picking a target audience and building your brand is an important part of the process, but we'll get into that in Chapters 13 to 20 of the book.

KEY TAKEAWAYS
Part 1: The Foundation

- Podcasts have become an increasingly popular method of storytelling, especially since 2014
- People are listening to podcasts and the numbers continue to grow
- Listeners are typically well educated and affluent
- Podcasts resonate with listeners and they are likely to making a purchase connected to what they're listening to
- Podcasts are making money by selling ads, based on the number of downloads

Part 2

WHAT'S OUT THERE?

Chapter 4

OVERALL STATS FROM CURRENT PODCASTS

There are tons of podcasts being released every day. For those who are regularly listening to podcasts, you may have already noticed that it can be overwhelming to keep up! Industry trends are always evolving, but let's get into some specific numbers from current podcasts.

Apple says iTunes has more than 250,000 unique podcasts in more than 100 languages. But many are short-lived. In 2015, the host of podcast The Plural of You, Josh Morgans, conducted a research project to learn more about podcast listening behaviours. According to his findings, "between June 2005 and June 2015, a typical podcast ran for six months and twelve episodes, at two episodes per month, before going inactive."

Most active podcasts by category? As of 2015, number one on the list was Christian-themed, with more than 20,000 different podcasts. Second was music and third was comedy. In 2015, podcasters added about 5,000 new podcasts to iTunes US per month.

So yeah, there's a lot. But don't worry, this doesn't mean you can't add to it. I don't like it when people claim the space is too saturated. In the following chapter, I outline what niche areas could use more content. In Chapter 5, I'll explain why I think you shouldn't be intimidated by the flux of people uploading content.

Chapter 5

FORMATS, GENRES & WHAT'S MISSING

Podcasting gives people free rein for formatting. Unlike radio, which has to fit to a clock, podcast formats range.

FORMATS

Common podcast formats that you'll hear include:

ONE PERSON SHOW

This is tough to pull off, but is typically done by comedians (who will essentially just do a standup act) or it will be done with a pre-written script with information someone wants to share.

CHAT CAST

Probably the most frequently heard. This is where two co-hosts will talk about a range of topics in a conversational style. They may incorporate audio if it relates to the given topic they're discussing or have on guests to be interviewed.

SERIALIZED

This is done in a journalistic style, where a story is told episode by episode. You will likely need to listen to the episodes in the order they are released. There isn't necessarily a resolution at the end of each episode, but each episode will highlight some sort of pivot in the story. All the episodes, together, will tell the story. This can be presented as a one-off mini series or continually, focusing on a different large story for each season.

THEMATIC SERIES

This is typically the type of podcast produced by national public radio (NPR) stations. They pick a theme to cover throughout a series, which are then organized into seasons. Episodes are standalone stories and can be listened to in any order. This is similar to current affairs programming that we're familiar with on TV. Themes are usually broad topics, like entrepreneurship, personal finance or matters of the heart.

VIGNETTES

These are short stories, rants or tips that can be grouped into an ongoing series or a mini-series. They are typically about 3 to 5 minutes long and highlight quick bites of information. This is an effective format for people who want to publish on a frequent basis. It's also a good way to get your feet wet with podcasting and experiment with audio storytelling.

GENRES

There are specific genres depending on topics (ie. religious based, music or lifestyle) but when I say genre, I'm talking about bigger buckets.

NEWS

This will include the topical headlines, interviews and maybe commentary. They are tailored to people who are digesting these as part of their regular routine and may want to download the podcast to listen to offline instead of streaming a radio station.

DOCUMENTARY

This genre will follow a non-fiction story, including a variety of angles, characters and information as it arises. This is done in a journalistic style where there is a team doing research and investigating a particular story.

EVERGREEN

This is one of the most common genres of successful podcasts. It provides information or a story that is not time sensitive. You can listen to this at any time and appreciate the content that is presented.

FICTIONAL

This is a scripted podcast that mimics original radio entertainment. All the voices are actors and the storylines will sometimes even include a reason for why they are being recorded in order to make it sounds more realistic. This format is especially popular in Spain, where they've started creating telenovela podcasts.

WHAT'S MISSING?

But people are continuing to experiment with genres and new ones are constantly emerging. For instance, the concept of a musical podcast was introduced in 2017 with the first ever fully-formed musical podcast, 36 Questions: a 3-act podcast musical with original soundtrack. Poetry and spoken word podcasts are also becoming increasingly popular.

With all these formats and genres, it's no surprise that there are loads of podcasts online and not nearly enough time to listen to them all. With this in mind, several networks have attempted to create a podcast that provides a round up of what's out there. One of the most notable ones was WAMU's The Big Listen, hosted by Lauren Ober. It ran from January 2016 until May 2018 and provided audiences with podcasts they may have never heard of and the inside scoop on popular ones that were dominating the charts. Lauren did a lot of listening and, in the fall of 2017, compiled a list of what's missing in the podcast space. Here's what was included:

- Shows featuring the following voices:
    - the very old & the very young
    - people who are not middle-class
    - female-identified people
- Audio fiction that is not about sci-fi
- History podcasts that are shorter, use more sound and are not about white European men
- Serialized narrative nonfiction featuring women's stories

This is not meant to sway you to creating a podcast that fits into one of these categories — it's more so meant to illustrate that despite the mass amount of podcasts available, there are still a lot of untapped areas that can be explored!

Chapter 6

LESSONS FROM NOTABLE PODCASTS

Let's take a look at some podcasts that have performed well. If you're able to take a listen to the episodes outlined below, that will allow for a better understanding of the formats being referred to. This is also a great list of podcasts to start with if you're new to the scene and don't know where to start.

SERIAL

Serialized: Documentary

Serial's first season has been mentioned earlier in this book — it's the podcast that became wildly popular and broke several Apple records. Even if you've heard the series before, try listening with a different lens. Take note of the scripting, the sound effects and the music. Here's a good place to start...

SEASON 1, EPISODE 1: THE ALIBI

The host, journalist Sarah Koenig, is reading from a script, but in a very conversational way. It's well written and in her "voice," which means it sounds natural for her to say. The story is told week-by-week in a sequential format where, just like most television series, it only makes sense if you watch it from the beginning and in the order that it is released. It's also journalistic in nature, where there are interview subjects and the host isn't an all-knowing expert. She's positioned herself as a character that is trying to uncover all the facts about the situation and there are no actors.

The podcast incorporates clips from the people she's speaking to, similar to how the news would package a story. Although the interviews she conducts are likely lengthy, she summarizes the main concepts in her narrative and then pairs it with clips, which are usually key statements that are worth highlighting. Hearing a variety of voices is important and spacing the clips out allows for it to be easier to listen to. Music also helps with keeping the listener engaged.

You'll notice music is used underneath her narrative throughout the script in the beginning. This can go unnoticed by the listener, but sets a mood for the story that's being told. The acoustic music doesn't sound terrifying or edgy, but allows for a more mysterious, curious tone. If you're not paying close attention, you might not even notice it. This is known as "driving music" which pushes the story along. We'll talk more about music choices in Chapter 17.

START UP

Serialized: Documentary

This is a podcast produced by Gimlet Media, chronicling what it's like to start a business in the United States. Season 1 follows Alex Blumberg as he develops his podcasting company, which you quickly learn is Gimlet Media. Yes, it's a podcast about starting a podcast. Very meta.

There will be more information about Gimlet Media in Chapter 9. For now, let's talk about their first episode, "How Not to Pitch a Billionaire".

SEASON 1, EPISODE 1: HOW NOT TO PITCH A BILLIONAIRE

The style of storytelling is similar to Serial, but in the first episode, there's a particular tactic that stands out to me. In the middle of this episode, you'll notice the host, Alex Blumberg, takes a long, raw, unscripted conversation (where he's pitching his company to a billionaire) and interjects it with scripted commentary. It's a layered style that combines that first wave of podcasting with the second wave. His scripted commentary does three things:

1. Provides context to parts of the conversation that the audience should know. This prevents the audience from feeling "left out" and quickly catches them up to speed, without having a long preamble to preface what they're about to hear.

2. Describes the scene and things that aren't captured through audio. For instance, he describes the investor's facial expressions and where they were standing on the street, in order for you to feel like you were right there with them. It paints a picture in the listener's mind.

3. Allows Alex to share internal thoughts, which makes it funny and lets the audience in on a more vulnerable side of the host. This is something that traditional radio hosts do quite often to bond with their listeners; a notable tactic of Howard Stern, who shared personal stories like his wife's miscarriage on the air, which increases his popularity.

ENVOY OFFICE HACKS

Vignettes: Evergreen

This is a branded podcast, funded by Envoy: a software company in San Francisco that makes visitor registration easy. So, with that theme in mind, they are creating content that highlights other stories from companies coming up for solutions in the workplace. Hence the title "Office Hacks."

SEASON 1, EPISODE 3: MICROWAVE OF SHAME

All the episodes are fairly short, and tell a full story in about five minutes or less. This makes it easy to "binge" listen.

It is journalistic in style, where the host goes into the office that is being featured, takes a look at the "hack" and asks questions along the way. There is a combination of clips: scripted narration, raw audio from the tour and clips of the interview subject explaining any additional information.

In this episode, they're talking about how their office tries to encourage a healthy lifestyle of eating fresh foods. This is why they've deemed it their "microwave of shame." The podcast uses an echo sound effect on the host when he says "microwave of shame," which is one way to keep it fun and prevent it from sounding drab (since there were limited additional sound effects that could complement the story). The narration is very descriptive, which helps the listeners envision what the microwave looks like and where it's placed. This makes them feel like they're "there."

This type of series is evergreen, meaning that it's not telling a story that will become dated. Envoy can easily continue this series and keep old episodes up on their website for listeners to enjoy at any time.

THE MESSAGE
Serialized: Fiction

This is a science fiction, branded podcast, paid for by General Electric. In Chapter 9 we'll take a closer look at its business strategy, but for now, let's talk about its format.

SEASON 1: TEASER EPISODE

The teaser (which is like a movie trailer for the podcast series) gives the audience a taste of what's to come in the series. You find out it's about a cryptology group trying to decode an alien message from the 1940's.

All the sounds are very intentional. In this sample, you'll hear there's a man's voice, which sounds like it was recorded over the phone. This was done on purpose to signify that it's a phone conversation, without explicitly explaining to the audience that the host was on a call.

Like many fictional series, The Message has written into the story why the "host" is recording everything. She's an intern creating a podcast. It's one way they've made it sound more believable for the listener.

Episodes in the series are about 15 minutes each.

MODERN LOVE
Thematic series: Evergreen

This podcast is based off the modern love section of the New York Times, which takes essay submissions from readers. The newspaper teamed up with Boston radio station WBUR to repurpose these essays.

SEASON 1 EPISODE 2: ONE LAST SWIRL

This episode is narrated by actor Jason Alexander and features the story by author Dan Barry. The essay talks about mortality and the death of Dan's pet fish. Jason reads the opening of the essay with music lightly in the background to help set the quirky, fun tone of the beginning of the piece. Throughout the essay light sound effects are used to highlight certain aspects, but the audience is very well aware that they are very intentional as they are added in after recording, similar to a fictional podcast.

The essay takes a turn in tone when Dan starts talking about the death of his mother. You'll notices the sounds and music change to reflect the shift. This initial format is similar to an audiobook, where the story is told in one voice, even if there are multiple characters. This is a great way to tell stories without interviews. This is also a great format to mimic if you are wanting to turn your blog into a podcast. Tweak the stories to be read aloud and record yourself (or an actress!) reading them.

After the actor finishes the reading, the podcast format changes and the host will interview the author and the editor of the Modern Love section. They will also feature a clip from the actor about why they felt connected to the essay. The interview portion is genuine and authentic, where people are speaking as themselves in an open and honest fashion. This is a great example of how you can mix fictional storytelling editing tactics and journalistic storytelling.

SLEEP WITH ME
One person show: Evergreen

This is an example of a niche podcast that is wildly successful because people rely on it to help them fall asleep. It features a man mumbling stories and lullabies. You can listen to any part of any episode for a few seconds to understand what it's like.

It's promoted as a "lulling, droning, boring, bedtime story to distract your racing mind." It is pre-scripted to a certain extent and the lullabies have light music underneath, but this is a case where having too much audio variety would be jarring to the listener and prevent them from falling asleep, so they intentionally do not use any sound effects.

This is also a great example of the type of audio content that would be difficult to add to programming for a traditional radio station, but is needed on-demand by a large audience.

WTF WITH MARC MARON
Chat cast: Evergreen/News

WTF (Waiting for the Punch) with Marc Maron is one of the notable "chat casts" that has been extremely successful. Marc has produced more than 800 episodes and made waves when he was able to interview President Barack Obama on the show in 2015.

This was not only a big moment for his show, but for podcasts as a whole, since it was now apparent that even the President of the United States and his staff acknowledged the power of reaching people through this medium.

Marc asks evergreen questions like "What do you do to have fun?" which would be interesting to hear, no matter when you listen. But also sprinkles in some questions about current events that would date the the podcast, which is why I've also classified it as news.

Overall, Marc takes a very conversational approach to his interviews and makes his audiences feel like they're in the conversation with him. He will have notes and bullets that he wants to hit upon, but the majority is not scripted, other than the opening introduction and closing "thank yous."

DINNER PARTY DOWNLOAD

Chat cast/Thematic series: News/evergreen

This is an American Public Media production that has two main hosts and then rotating guests who pop in during different segments. For instance in Episode 373 they have on Rachel Bloom, Steve Aoki, James Baldwin.

The podcast is about an hour long and is broken up into segments that are tied together under the theme of the dinner party, but aren't actually connected with one straightforward storyline. This is why the podcast differentiates each segment by giving it a title (ie. The icebreaker, small talk, cocktails, etc).

Transitions in this podcast are scripted, and so are some of the fact-driven segments, which is more like a thematic series. But then, they insert long interview clips, which are unscripted, and aligns more with a chat cast. This is a great example of how you can mix a variety of formats.

They also mix genres. The small talk segment is done with audio montages of news items and interviews with subject matter experts. This would be classified as news.

Right after that, you heard the cocktails segment, which had two components: a historical story (which was scripted and done like a traditional news report) and the drink that it inspires (which was pre-planned but not scripted and done with the host and an expert). Technically, this piece is evergreen and enjoyed at any time.

No matter how you classify it, it's extremely well produced and slickly edited. Each of the segments have loads of audio variety. You'll notice lots of music, sound effects and even accent audio (like bells and dings). The two hosts carry you through the entire episode, but different voices are weaved in to carry different segments.

Like traditional radio, there are teasers at the beginning of the episode to give people a taste of what's ahead, with the hopes of keeping them listening for the entire show. It's also very fast-paced, which is similar to many news wheel radio stations.

Chapter 7

AD STYLES & BEST PRACTICES

Podcasting has not only expanded the way that people are telling audio stories — it's changed the way that audio ads are being created. Here are some notable ad formats and examples of each.

Before we dive in, I would like to stipulate: when I use the word "produced" in the style formats here, it means that there was a script, likely some sort of storyboard and the ad was heavily edited.

PRODUCED WITH EXTERNAL VOICE

This style is most closely aligned with a traditional radio ad. The podcast host says they're going to take a break, a new (usually unnamed) voice comes on and starts saying an ad. Living Proof is one company who has ads like this in the podcast Modern Love. They incorporate the ad narrator reading referrals about their hair products, and then articulate a call to action for audiences. In this case, it's for them to go to the website and use a promo code specific to the podcast.

Note: Using promo codes specific to your podcast is a great way for you (and your clients) to get an idea of how your audiences are responding to the ads.

PRODUCED WITH INTERNAL VOICE

This is when an ad company commissions their ad directly from the podcast. This usually happens when there's an organization or production team working on the podcast. A great example is the original sponsor of Serial, which was Mail Chimp. It was made by Serial producers Dana Chivvis and Julie Snyder and featured a series of random voices talking about Mail Chimp and reading parts of the script. To be be creative, they left in some of the raw audio (for instance, when someone stumbled and said Mail "Kimp" instead of Chimp). When the podcast took off, so did the ad for Mail Chimp. People loved the accidental mispronunciation and took to social media by storm. Mail Chimp capitalized on this and even bought the domain MailKimp.com.

Another important piece to note about the production of this ad is the raw audio that they included at the end. It's of one of the producers saying off mic "I use Mail

Chimp" and the other responds, "Do you?" and it trails off. This touch adds a layer of authenticity and has listeners make the connection between the voices they're hearing in the show and the product that is being sold.

LIVE READS

This will be a script or bullets that is provided by the client to the host. The ad is not prerecorded or edited, the host will just do the ad live at some point in the podcast. This is the easiest to incorporate and the client/podcaster can come to an agreement about how much flexibility there is with the script or bullets given. The most successful ads are the ones that allow the host to insert their personality into the read.

Comedian Bill Burr got lots of attention with his live reads for Me Undies. There are edited compilations of his live reads that have gone viral online. He's authentic and opens with unscripted lines like "Let's read a little

QUICK TIP

Live reads should still sound natural and authentic to the host's voice. If you're attempting to do this style of ad yourself, make sure you are comfortable with the script and it's written in a way that honours the tone of your podcast.

advertising here for this Thursday afternoon..." and then goes on to read the bullets but also mock the company. As a comedian, it works!

Nazanin Rafsanjani is creative director at Gimlet Media and oversees their ad creation and branded content. Speaking at the 2017 Werk It podcast conference, she outlined four ingredients to make a good ad:

- Employs the same storytelling techniques you use to make a good podcast episode
- Has a beginning, middle and end
- Finds a sweet spot in terms of length
- Is authentic to the show

The moral is that ad creation needs just as much love as you'd put into creating the podcast, itself. And, just like podcasts, there is no one "right" way of doing it. There's a lot of room for creativity and exploration.

🔑 KEY TAKEAWAYS
Part 2: What's Out There?

- There are a lot of podcasts being produced, but many aren't actively publishing
- There is a lot of flexibility with podcast formats (ie. one person show, chat cast, serialized, etc)
- There are also a lot of different genres for podcasts (ie. evergreen, fictional, news, etc)
- Listening to some of the more successful podcasts will give you an idea of what works
- Podcast ads are an art in themselves

Part 3

WHAT'S NEXT?

Chapter 8

THE RISE OF THE PODCAST CELEBRITY

You may hear people criticize podcasting as a medium because "there's so much out there" and "who has time to listen to it all?" Fair. But let's remember a medium with similar trajectory.

Think back to when YouTube first launched in 2005. It blew up. In its first year, 8 million videos were being watched each day. By 2006, 65,000 videos were being uploaded per day. In 2018, nearly 5 billion videos are watched every day and 300 hours of video are uploaded to YouTube every minute. Yes, in the beginning, much that was being uploaded was low quality and it was impossible to digest it all. But as this experimentation process was underway, people became increasingly talented at producing videos and "YouTube celebrities" emerged.

Now there are people who make a living because of their regular video creation and dedicated following. Brands are looking to work with these "influencers" all the time. YouTube as a platform allows these content creators to make money through ad sales on the platform.

Why would the podcasting space be any different? Perhaps it's unrolling at a bit of a slower pace, but stages are parallel. Here are the phases, as I see it:

- The experimentation phase with an abundance of content
- The rise of quality content
- The emergence of the celebrity content creator
- The advertisers who want to buy in
- The brands that try to create their own

(and all throughout)

- The evolution of the platform to keep the content coming

Which ultimately leads to an uphill trajectory of more content, more audiences and more money.

Right now, podcasting is in the thralls of the messy middle where there are celebrities starting to emerge, curious advertisers, and many companies deciding whether or not they should take the plunge in investing properly to create their own, which brings me to my next chapter.

> 🔍 **DID YOU KNOW?**
>
> Megan Tan is an example of a "podcast celebrity" who published the first episode of Millennial in 2014, thinking it would just be for her friends and family to listen to. Within three years it went from being a passion project to a full-time job, garnering up to 400k downloads per month.

Chapter 9

THE FUTURE OF BRANDED PODCASTS

According to the Content Marketing Institute, "Content marketing is a strategic marketing approach focused on creating and distributing valuable, relevant, and consistent content to attract and retain a clearly-defined audience — and, ultimately, to drive profitable customer action."

That's exactly what companies like Shopify are trying to do. Tucker Schreiber, product manager for Shopify, said at the 2016 Social Media Week in Toronto: "We'd rather be the entertainment rather than the interruption." He was referring to their podcast, called TGIM: The Essential Podcast for Ambitious Entrepreneurs. They hired Pacific Content to create episodes and release them every other week.

Creating a podcast as a top-of-funnel marketing tactic is becoming an increasingly popular way of reaching new audiences. It's the entire model for the company that created TGIM. They strategically help create podcasts with key messaging that aligns with brands without going overboard with ads. The TGIM podcast doesn't even have a full liner advertising Shopify. Just a quick "from Shopify" at the beginning and another brief mention at the end.

The flexibility with podcasts as part of a content marketing strategy is that it can be a top of funnel piece for one person, but a different part of the funnel for others. Brands have the option of releasing episodes in advance to current users or offering extra bonus episodes as a "thank you."

Pacific Content has also created podcasts for companies like Slack, Envoy (which we looked at in the previous chapter) and Mozilla. They argue that there's a huge gap between mobile usage and ad spending there, mostly because research shows that people skip ads.

Their solution?

"Make great content that people actually want to engage with. Content gives the consumer control to consume what they do and do not want, without interruptions. The only trick for brands is that your content has to be fantastic to get noticed."

And how do you do that? By telling good stories. Audiences are looking for content that is authentic, engaging and useful.

> ### 💡 QUICK TIP
>
> Take a page from Pacific Content's playbook:
>
> - Make sure that you're producing ads that people actually want to engage with
> - When it comes to getting noticed, your best bet is to produce extraordinary content

It's the type of storytelling that Gimlet Media was doing when they started getting approached by companies who wanted them to create branded podcasts. Gimlet launched in 2014 and within two years had more than six different shows and more than 50 employees. We looked at a sample of their first series in the previous chapter.

In order to keep their brand as a podcast company authentic, they launched a separate arm for branded podcasts called Gimlet Creative. They boast that they create "highly produced narrative audio in partnership with brands. Our integrated ad campaigns and branded shows are made by some of the best audio producers in the business." They've produced podcasts for brands like Tinder and EBay.

According to AdWeek, EBay's Open for Business "landed in the No. 1 spot for business podcasts in iTunes when it launched in June 2016." They also said it reached more than 200 percent of its download goal.

Panoply is a network that dabbles in both curating and creating podcasts. They have created branded podcasts for companies like Purina and General Electric.

Their sci-fi branded podcast for GE made waves as it was one of the recent fictional podcasts to top the charts. The Message had one season with eight episodes. It follows a character named Nicky Tomalin who is documenting a cryptology group that is decoding a message sent from (what is believed to be) aliens.

The podcasts themselves don't mention GE, but on the website where it's hosted, the disclaimer reads, "The medical technology and treatments in this podcast are fictional, but to learn more about the real technology that GE is working on in the ultrasound therapy space, visit..."

The result? A number one rated podcast with more than one million listeners.

Chapter 10

PODCASTS GOING TO LIVE AUDIENCES

Podcasts are known for allowing listeners to have an intimate experience with the host and content, but an emerging trend is to perform podcasts live. It's where filming TV shows in front of a live audience meets the fluidity of a concert. Audience members are encouraged to react, with all audio being captured for the release of the episode, but the podcast rolls through without stopping or doing any retakes. Some of the first podcasters to go "on tour" with their podcasts were comedians, who were basically doing a giant bit as their podcast, so recording while performing live was a natural fit.

More complicated performances are from journalistic story-tellers who need additional producers on stage with them to play clips and cue music (which is also sometimes performed live).

With live podcast performances came festivals who were interested in incorporating these recordings. Just For Laughs Toronto has hosted many comedians whose performances were being recorded as episodes for their podcast and were promoted accordingly. Another mainly comedy-focused podcast festival is the LA Podcast Festival, which was founded in 2012.

Podcasts focused on journalistic storytelling have also started to gather for festivals. Toronto hosted its first ever Hot Docs Podcast Festival in 2016 and included several live performances, panel discussion and networking events. It's been running annually ever since.

Events dedicated to podcast networking and professional development have also been popping up, including WNYC's Werk It, which brings together women working in audio and digital media. One of the most popular audio conferences is the Third Coast Conference in Chicago. Since 2001, they've been bringing together radio producers, podcasters and audio artists to listen to each other's work, take part in workshops and network.

🔎 DID YOU KNOW?

Podcast companies like Midroll are starting to invest in staff members who focus specifically on event planning.

Chapter 11

PODCAST AWARDS

With the rise of high quality podcasts comes acknowledgment! In addition to digital awards being given to podcasts, legacy media awards are expanding their categories to include podcasting. Here are some of the popular awards that are recognizing excellence in podcasting.

RTDNA

Canada's Radio Television Digital News Association added a podcasting category for their 2018 awards ceremony for the best "single podcast or a podcast series which displays an outstanding use of the aural medium."

PEABODY AWARDS

This is an American-based award known for highlighting excellence in storytelling. It's one of the most prestigious podcasting awards to receive and has several sub-categories like best single episode, nest narrative series and best news programming.

WEBBY AWARDS

This award show honours the best of the internet and not only has its own podcast, but gives out awards for the best branded podcast, best podcast host, best individual episode and best series.

There are also specific national award ceremonies popping up, like the British Podcast Awards and the Australian Podcast Awards, which both launched in 2017.

DID YOU KNOW?

In 2014, Serial became the first-ever podcast to win a Peabody award.

Chapter 12

WHO TO KEEP AN EYE ON

The podcast scene is rapidly expanding and there are always rumblings about what the major players have on the horizon. Just like the coach of a varsity sports team, I've started keeping my eye on some of the prospects that can change the game as we know it. From talking to people within the industry, I've curated a roster of promising players. Here is a list of notable companies and departments that I'm keen to follow (and why):

PINEAPPLE STREET MEDIA

They're a podcast production house that is known for creating shows like Missing Richard Simmons and Women of the Hour with Lena Dunham. One of the people to thank for all its brilliance so far is Jenna Weiss-Berman, who was formally the director of audio for BuzzFeed. The company is expanding and looking to continue to produce non-fiction mini series. They have also been known to collaborate with Stitcher.

STITCHER

A site and app known for hosting podcasts. It has recently been acquired by Midroll Media (which was a company that originally focused on pairing advertisers with podcasters). They are now creating original content and developing the audio hosting aspects of the app. I've been told there are big changes to come.

NPR PODCASTS (KIDS & FAMILY)

I believe podcasts for kids is a huge market and NPR's department is the leader in the space. They produce content that is great for kids, but interesting for parents to listen to as well. They have shows like *But Why: A Podcast for Curious Kids* and *Wow in the World*. I also have heard they are expecting to expand their roster.

GLOBE AND MAIL

One of Canada's national newspapers has been dabbling in the podcast scene and is set to be investing in a big way, especially for a newspaper. Their first official series (launched in September 2016) was called *Colour Code* and covered the topic of race in Canada. Since then, the Globe and Mail has commissioned research in Canadian podcast listening habits (see results in Chapter 2) and is exploring the idea of expanding their podcast offerings.

CORUS

The Canadian media and broadcast company (known for its radio and television properties), hired its first-ever director of streaming and podcasting in 2018. They're growing a podcasting team in order to leverage internal content and external talent in order to build a high-quality audio network.

VOCAL FRY STUDIOS

This is an inclusive Toronto podcast studio and community workspace that offers access to podcasting workshops and production support. They are determined to work with people from underrepresented groups. I'm excited to see what will be developed out of this space and how it will impact the Canadian podcast landscape.

HOW TO KEEP UP WITH THE LATEST PODCAST NEWS?

One of the most popular podcast newsletters right now is produced by Nick Quah. He used to work for Business Insider and BuzzFeed but is now single-handedly keeping the podcast community up to date with his Hot Pod Newsletter. He talks jobs, acquisitions and new releases. He also gets a bit gossipy sometimes about big players in the game and I love it. You can sign up for it at www.hotpodnews.com.

Another great resource is in the New Yorker. Staff writer Sarah Larson writes a column called Podcast Dept and includes reviews, releases and commentary about the podcast industry.

Although both are American sources, they keep a close eye on the Canadian market as well and incorporate updates accordingly. Also, paying attention to the American market is only going to be indicative of what's to come for the industry as a whole, so I think it's worth taking note.

For more technical updates, a Canadian podcast blog I'm a fan of is Pacific Content's blog.pacific-content.com. I referenced one of their blogs in the first chapter of this book and I continue to look to them for the latest on product developments, marketing tips and general podcasting fun facts.

QUICK TIP

Sign up for a podcast newsletter to help you stay on top of industry trends both at home and abroad.

For more of an international perspective (and if you're ready to commit to daily podcast news), you can sign up for the PodNews.net newsletter. It's promoted as being "Your daily briefing for podcasting and on-demand." The guy behind it is James Cridland, who is a consultant out of Australia, but used to work in the United Kingdom.

🗝 KEY TAKEAWAYS
Part 3: What's Next?

- Get ready for the rise of the podcast celebrity, similar to the YouTube trajectory
- Expect to see more branded podcasts as part of content marketing strategies
- Podcasts are now being brought to live audiences
- There is an increasing number of awards that recognize excellence in podcasting
- If you want to stay on top of all the latest podcast news, there are several newsletters, blogs and journalists dedicated to covering the podcast beat

Part 4

DOING IT YOURSELF

Chapter 13

STARTING YOUR OWN PODCAST

By now you're hopefully excited by the realm of possibilities with podcasting and are considering if you should take the plunge and start your own. Although you may want to grab your phone and hit record, here are some important things to nail down right off the bat:

PICK A NICHE TOPIC THAT'S ALSO YOUR PASSION

Don't try to be everything to everyone. The beauty of podcasts is that you can drill in on very specific topics and resonate with a key audience. Then you can find advertisers accordingly. Highlight your expertise or start telling stories in a way that hasn't been done yet. As you've read, there's already a lot of content out there, so you want something that is going to stand out.

WHAT WILL BE YOUR FORMAT?

The best way to inform your decision for a format is to listen to a variety of formats (see Chapter 5 for a list of formats/genres and Chapter 6 for examples of what's out there). Pick one that will suit the content you plan to share. For instance, if you're wanting to turn your blog into a podcast, it might be beneficial to format it similarly to the way the New York Times created a podcast from their Modern Love section: getting an actor to read each story (with accompanying sound effects) and then having a short discussion afterward about the theme.

HAVE A BUDGET IN MIND

It's easy to get overwhelmed with all the production options available for podcasters. Pick a budget and then find the equipment and software that fits what you're willing to invest. There are more details on this in the next two chapters.

QUICK TIP

Don't try to be everything to everyone.

TIPS FROM ANNA SALE

The opening remarks at the 2017 Werk It podcast conference for women were from Anna Sale, the host of Death, Sex & Money from WNYC Studios. She listed 10 tips (plus a bonus!) to help people who are getting into the world of podcasting. Here are her bullets with a little commentary from me.

#1 LISTEN TO YOUR RESTLESSNESS

What story or topic makes you get fired up? Follow that. Take note of what you're passionate about and what message you're itching to share with the world. That's the fuel you need to drive your podcast.

#2 GET CLOSE TO PEOPLE DOING WHAT YOU WANT TO DO

Is there a podcast you like, or a company producing content that you think is great? Reach out. Talk to them. Shadow them. Absorb as much as you can!

#3 PRACTISE (EVEN IF YOU DON'T KNOW WHAT TO MAKE)

People can easily get up in their heads about all the nitty gritty details. I get it. There's a lot to consider before launching a podcast. But don't be afraid to just start. Play with the mic, practice recording, try your hand at editing. You don't have to publish everything you produce. Go in with an exploratory mindset. And hey, you might be pleasantly surprised with what you make and then you can decide later if you want to share it more widely.

#4 GET EDITED

Whether or not you publish your first pieces, be sure to strategically share them with people who can give you feedback. Send it to anyone in your network who regularly listens to podcasts and/or anyone you know who works in the podcasting industry. Ask for feedback on the overall content, the pacing, tone, music, editing, etc. Even the most established podcasts have an extensive review process. When you're too close to the content, it's hard to objectively go back and listen to your own work.

#5 FACE THE REALITY YOU'RE LEARNING IN PUBLIC

Publishing your first episode can be nerve-wracking but it's normal to feel that way. Remember that your first episode will not be perfect and your podcast will evolve as you continue to create episodes. That's ok.

#6 ASK: WHAT'S FEEDING YOU? WHAT'S DEPLETING YOU?

As you're putting together your podcast, be aware of the process and what parts you're passionate about. Ask yourself, what part of this is feeding me and what part of this is depleting me? Do you like voicing? Or does the thought of nailing the delivery stress you out? Is editing exciting or frustrating? Once you get over the initial learning hump (where everything might be a bit overwhelming) you can start to zero in on what parts you want to continue to do and what parts you may want to outsource. Podcasting should be fun and "feed" you, not "deplete" you!

#7 ACCEPT INVITATIONS

Be open to collaborating with other podcasters! A lot of podcasters grow their listenership from being featured on other podcasts. Teaming up with other people in the industry is common practice and can lead to regular crossovers or partnerships.

#8 MAKE THE SHOW YOU NEED

Is there a topic that's been weighing on your heart? Follow that. Authenticity shows. Making something that is true to you and your passions will be evident. And rest assured there are others out there that are similar to you.

#9 ASK: WHY DOES THE WORLD NEED *THIS* PODCAST?

If you have an idea for a podcast, do some research before you start recording. Is there anything else similar out there? What makes yours different? Do you have a unique angle to a topic or story? Or is there a topic that isn't being covered in all its fullness? Try not to overpopulate the medium with duplicate content. If you need some ideas on what we're lacking, revisit Chapter 5.

#10 ASK: WHAT DO I NEED TO DO THIS WELL?

You don't need to purchase the full suite of high-end equipment to make a high quality podcast, but you *do* need to put some thought into what will provide a strong foundation and invest accordingly. For instance, if you've decided to go with a podcast format that has you conducting interviews, you'll want to make sure you have a microphone that is meant for two people.

BONUS: PASS IT ON!

As you go on this podcast journey, you're going to learn a lot. Share what you've learned. This is an exploratory time and we want to share knowledge and help build the podcasting community.

Chapter 14

PRODUCTION EQUIPMENT

If you're wanting to create a podcast on your own and are looking to invest on the basic equipment to get started, this chapter is for you. Doing the work yourself gives you complete creative control and helps you learn about the art of audio storytelling.

MICROPHONE BASICS

First, let's break down the different styles of microphones there are. This will inform what kind of recorder you purchase.

- **Omni-directional**: captures audio equally from all directions. This is good if you're trying to capture sound from an event where all sound are important (ie. a rally, where you want to hear a lot of overlapping voices, chants, etc).

- **Cardioid**: captures audio mainly from what is directly in front of the mic and a little bit on each side, but not what's directly behind it. This is great if you are positioning it in front of a person who is moving around while they're speaking.

- **Hyper-cardioid/directional**: captures the audio of mostly what is directly in front of the mic and a little bit from directly behind it. This is the type of microphone that a lot of reporters will use when interviewing subjects with high quality in addition to capturing their own questions for context (but not as a priority).

- **Figure 8**: captures audio equally from the front and the back. This is great for someone sitting down for an interview and both parties want to be captured equally. This type of microphone is usually very valuable for podcasters.

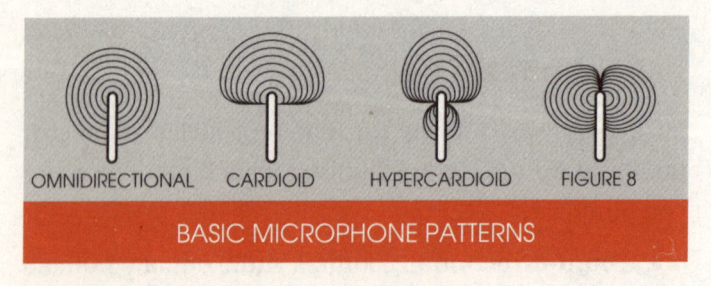

BASIC MICROPHONE PATTERNS

ABOVE *black lines show how each microphone captures audio.*

> ## 💡 QUICK TIP
>
> Before you start buying a bunch of equipment, set an approximate budget for yourself. Stick to what you're comfortable with in the beginning and then add on as you become more sophisticated with your production process.

RECORDING

There are a lot of recorders out there and it can be overwhelming to choose, even for seasoned professionals. Different types of recorders suit different methods of capturing audio. Ultimately you need two components: a microphone and somewhere to record to. Some microphones will have recording capabilities built in. Your other option is to purchase a recording device plus a microphone that you would connect.

Think about the type of podcast you want to create, how you will be collecting audio most of the time, and what types of equipment you're comfortable with.

If you're going to be static and recording from home, or in an office, then something like one of the Blue Microphones would be ideal. They offer models that plug into your phone or your computer in order to record. Many of their models allow you to switch the recorder's microphone style. For instance, the Yeti offers all four types of microphones listed in the previous section!

If you're looking to do a lot of recording in the field, it's ideal to get a microphone and recorder that's an all-in-one unit so you don't have to bring along a laptop to record. A great start is investing in Zoom Microphones. They record to SD cards and are easily portable. The H2 is perfect for beginners who still want a professional sound. One of their higher-end models is the H5, which allows you to change the microphone on the top according to your recording needs.

Zoom also offers add-on mics for phones, which can record both as a directional and as a figure 8.

Overall, it's good to invest in equipment that allows you to add on to it with different pieces. It gives you the flexibility to scale up in the future if your needs shift.

HEADPHONES

Headphones are key when recording. They allow you to monitor what your recording will sound like. A plane in the background? You might not notice it while you're interviewing someone, but it might be significantly more prominent in your recording. By wearing headphones, you'll be able to have the experience of the listener. Any over-the-ear headphone will suffice. Middle range ones tend to cost about $50-$150 and are perfectly fine to use whether you're a beginner or a pro.

If you're overwhelmed by all the options, try going with the Sony MDR 7506. They're great middle-range headphones that work well for mixing and editing. Chris Boyce (who so kindly wrote the foreword of this book!), swears by them. He told me he used them for his first job at the CBC 25 years ago and still uses them today. Timeless!

APPS AND RECORDING SYSTEMS

Ringr and Tape a Call are great for recording conversations on cell phones. Ringr is known for having a higher quality since it uses each phone's microphone to record the voice on each end, then mixes it together. Note that both people need the app. With Tape a Call, the quality is sacrificed but it's an easier system to use. You call the app on a third line and it simply records the call. You can then email a link to the audio file to yourself or save the audio file directly to your device.

Hindenburg allows for some of the highest quality for recording calls over the computer. It also allows you to monitor levels while you're recording and edit within the recording system. And the bonus is you can also use it for editing after you've recorded! You can get a free 30-day trial to test it out if you're unsure about investing.

Chapter 15

RECORDING TECHNIQUES

There are varying best practices for recording, depending on your format and how many people you are looking to record. Here are some general tips.

SINGLE VOICE RECORDING

If you are recording a voiceover, reading a script, or overseeing a single voice that will be recorded, you will want to be in a studio or small room. Many podcasts are recorded in small rooms (or even closets!) and you can't tell the difference. For an even crisper sound, you can record with a large blanket over your head and microphone. This is not ideal for long reads, but can mimic the sound of a studio recording. Speaking about three to four inches away from the microphone is what's recommended and the point of the mic that should be in front of your mouth will depend on the microphone you're using/the setting you have chosen. Be sure to take note of this before you start recording.

INTERVIEWS/DISCUSSIONS

Most of the tips for single voice recording also apply for recording interviews and discussions. The only difference is the microphone set up. You will want to make sure that all speakers are being captured, but you also want to make sure everyone feels comfortable with where they're physically sitting. For instance, if two people are being recorded, it's ideal for them to be sitting across from each other (rather than side by side) and speaking into a mic that is recording from both sides, or speaking into their own individual microphones.

QUICK TIP

Ensuring there's no background sound is important no matter where you're recording (unless of course, the background sound is intentional and part of the story).

LIVE TAPE

The wonderful thing about podcasts is that they can put the listener in any environment with just audio.

From a production standpoint, many struggle with capturing authentic audio for scene setters. Despite the lean equipment load that comes along with only capturing audio, people still become hyper-aware when they're being recorded. Here are a few tactics to help subjects feel comfortable as you record natural sound/live tape:

#1 ANSWER QUESTIONS IN ADVANCE

Many times people will have questions about the project or the equipment. Let them ask all of their questions before you start recording. Even let them examine the equipment. Kids especially appreciate having an opportunity to get a closer look.

#2 START ROLLING EARLY

Start rolling as soon as you can. Although you might think there's no use for any of the audio, it allows for the subjects to feel more at ease with what's happening. That way, by the time the valuable sounds start to happen, they've already become immersed in what they're doing and are not focusing on the fact that they're being recorded.

#3 TAKE A STEP BACK

Literally. If you choose the right equipment, you won't have to be directly in front of your subject, holding the microphone two inches from their face. That's intimidating for everyone, including professionals. Try to keep up with the action, while not being in the forefront. Remember that you can read more about equipment choices in the previous chapter.

#4 RECORD IMPORTANT SOUNDS TWICE

It's great to be able to rely on the original sound, but there are a few important sounds that you should make an effort to capture more than once because you know you'll need it for the finished product. Remember: it's not imperative that the re-record happens the very moment the initial sound takes place. When in doubt, don't disrupt the flow of action, but get the subject to make the sound again at the end of the recording or during a break.

#5 LEAVE IN THE MESSY PARTS

If you want it to sound natural, you have to leave in some of the parts that may sound "messy." A sneeze with a little reaction or the sound of a misstep will add to the authentic feel of the podcast.

Chapter 16

SCRIPTING 101

All podcasts require some sort of script. Even with a conversational chat cast, it's important to have intentional opening and closing scripts on each episode. So let's start there.

OPENING

Common practice is to jump right in. Introduce the name of your podcast and one sentence describing what it's about. Make sure this is eye level and that your listeners will understand what they're getting themselves into. Introduce yourself and any co-hosts you may have. You can also add to the opening by teasing what's to come in the episode (some like to do this by sharing clips of segments to follow). Here's a sample opening script for a podcast I created:

> *"A Pitch for Change is a podcast about what it takes to create a successful business that also has a positive social impact. I'm Amanda Cupido. In this episode..."*

CLOSING

List off the production team, their roles and any other acknowledgements that particular episode may require. Tease what's coming up in the next episode if possible. Using a clip from it is ideal. This will help listeners come back, or click to the next episode if it's already been released. Have your hosts sign off and then point to a website, or any other call to action that makes sense for your podcast. It may just be pointing to a place like iTunes for more episodes or asking them to rate the show.

Here's a sample closing script from the same podcast mentioned above:

> *"Coming up in the next episode [insert clip here]. A Pitch for Change is a production of [insert company here]. I'm Amanda Cupido, the producer and editor of the podcast, alongside [insert name here]. Sound mixing is by [insert name here]. [Insert name here] and [insert name here] are advisors to the show. For pictures of [insert name here] from this episode, you can visit www.[insert website here].com."*

> **QUICK TIP**
>
> When in doubt, listen to your favourite podcast and mimic the way they have scripted their opening and closing.

MIDDLE

As for everything in the middle — if you're going to be doing a chat cast and don't want to script the bulk of your podcast, I would still encourage you to put together an outline with scripted transitions. This will keep the flow somewhat in order and help everyone involved stay on the right track.

If you are planning to go for a more journalistic style of scripting and narration throughout the entire podcast, here are some bullets to keep in mind, especially if you're going to be writing it for yourself to read.

#1 WRITE TO YOUR VOICE

Use words that you would use in your everyday interactions. Don't try to get yourself to say things that don't sound natural to you. If you continually stumble on a specific word, change it. If you prefer to say "bucks" rather than "dollars," follow that instinct! It should sound like you're talking to a friend. If you find you're hitting a roadblock, call a friend and tell them the story. Don't overthink it. Just talk. Then use the way you retold it as inspiration for how to write your script.

#2 KEEP YOUR SENTENCES TIGHT

Don't try to have too many ideas in one sentence. Writing for the ear is different than writing for the eye. We can't digest as much information audibly and it's hard to read long sentences out loud. Keep your sentences short. Like this one.

#3 DON'T USE FIVE DOLLAR WORDS

This goes hand-in-hand with keeping your sentences tight. For the same reason, you don't want to overwhelm audiences with words that they need to process or think about extensively in order to understand the meaning. Write in an eye-level fashion that will be relatable. If there's a term that needs to be used in order to cover your story properly, explain the definition. It's important to make sure you don't lose your audience because of your vocabulary choices.

#4 CALL OUT THE OBVIOUS

If a clip that just played was a bit confusing (but you think it's important to include for the story), call it out in the script. ie. "I know that sounded confusing, but it's important because..." Or if a guest is sounding raspy but you need to conduct the interview, incorporate it into the podcast. Add another bullet in your outline and ask why their voice is raspy and how they're making it work.

#5 WRITE AND REWRITE

You may find the first time you write your script, you're bogged down by information and details. Don't be afraid to leave it and then revisit for a rewrite. Or to rewrite after you've tried recording. I've commonly rewritten scripts on the fly as I was recording because I found myself finding the words when I was in front of the mic. Give yourself the space and flexibility to do that.

Chapter 17

POST PRODUCTION

The time and energy spent on post production for your podcast may vary. For instance, chat casts (that are recorded as if they are live) typically take minimal time to edit, whereas serialized podcasts are a completely different story (in fact, most of the time spent creating these is during post production). Here's a look at each aspect of the post production process and tips for execution.

EDITING

Audacity is a free editing software that allows you to do the basics. Garage Band on Macs can also provide the same sort of simple editing.

More advanced editing software like Adobe Audition, ProTools or WavePad is good to invest in if you want to do more sophisticated edits and noise removal.

The best way to learn how to edit is to watch online tutorials (depending on what software you end up going with) and then practising!

MUSIC AND INDENTS

HOW TO ACQUIRE MUSIC

Music is a key component for your podcast. You can download royalty-free music, pay for licensed songs or compose your own.

You can find royalty free music online, like from Bensound, which just requires credit given at the end or FreeMusicArchive.org.

A great place to start for licensed music is Audio Jungle. They offer fairly low-priced music, often in "packs," which gives you a variety of different songs of similar nature that would fit well within a series. They also offer sound effects that can help add a bit of audio variety to your podcast (if you weren't able to record a certain sound yourself).

If you are going to be needing a lot of music, it may also be worth investing in a yearly subscription to services like Audio Jungle or APM Music.

Working with a composer is great for customized music and you can get variations of each song, including the original track, underscores, stems (which is the melody from each individual instrument) and a sting (which is at the end). If you are working with a composer, it's good to have an idea of what kind of music you're looking for them to compose. Put together a playlist of songs you want them to use as inspiration so that you can ensure you're on the same page. It's also important to stipulate within your working contract how many rounds of revisions you're expecting from them and what the final deliverables should include.

HOW TO CHOOSE YOUR MUSIC

Once you know where you are going to get your music from, you can now scan their selections and choose which ones are going to make it into your podcast. Don't kid yourself, this is an art.

The opening track sets the pace, tone and feel. Start by writing adjectives or verbs that match the vibe you are going for with your podcast. Your music throughout the entire podcast should match or have some sort of through-line with this initial track. The music you choose for your opening and closing is your identifying music that your audience will come to associate with the podcast. Choose wisely.

How you incorporate music off the top will be dependant on your song choice and opening scripting, but ideally you will let it play for at least 3-5 seconds off the top. You then will want it running under your opening and slowly fade out. You can have it running very low in the background for as long as you see fit. Even having it for up to a minute is fine, if you think it fits the pacing.

The same goes for the end. You can have it creep in as soon as you feel that it works. Just know that it will trigger the audience to knowing it's coming to a close, so you don't want to have it come in too early as it will throw listeners off. Have it running for the final thoughts and throughout the entire closing, where you will have your host sign off and include any credits or teases for upcoming episodes.

HOW TO INCORPORATE ADDITIONAL MUSIC THROUGHOUT

Incorporating the right music all throughout is also important to maintain the pacing, and can act as an accent to the content. In addition to your opening identifying music, many podcasts will also incorporate driving music. This is used throughout the podcast to bridge ideas, or add momentum to a topic that is being covered. This music should help bring the story to life.

This can take a lot of trial and error. You never know how music will change a story until you hear it play-

> **QUICK TIP**
>
> The best way to learn how to edit is to watch online tutorials (depending on what software you end up going with) and then practising!

ing underneath. Let yourself experiment with different songs and be creative. For instance, with fictional podcasts, it can be used as a motif. A certain song can play every time a specific character comes into the scene. In a documentary style podcast, if a character is being melodramatic, you can use a violin track, which can be comedic for audiences.

There is no right or wrong, but it's important to determine your own style and then maintain that throughout the series.

MUSICAL INDENTS AND LOGOS

A musical indent or logo is a sound effect that can be used like punctuation and associated with your brand. It can be a something as simple as a "ding" that is at the end of every podcast episode, but also used beyond just podcasts and incorporated into the endings of videos or traditional ads. If you're looking to create a full-fledged musical identity for your brand, this is an important piece you'll want to consider as part of your branding strategy, which brings me to my next section...

BRANDING

Using keywords to indicate what your podcast is about (especially in the description section upon uploading) is key. Remember, audio is not searchable on Google. So try to use words that explicitly indicate the podcast's subject matter in the title and/or supporting text areas.

ABOVE *an example of podcast artwork.*

With regard to visuals, all you'll need is a thumbnail that can supplement your audio files. Typically a square, sized 1400 x 1400 pixels. Don't underestimate the power of a powerful thumbnail. Call Your Girlfriend podcast producers have learned through surveying their audience that they gained listeners who simply clicked to listen because they thought their artwork was "cool." Another suggestion is to always include a transcript with every episode online. Not only does this make the content accessible, but it allows for search engine optimization.

UPLOADING

There are two steps involved in uploading your podcast and making it available for people to listen.

1. **Upload your audio files to a place that will store/**

host your podcast episodes. This can be on sites like SoundCloud (which is free, but also used for more than just podcasts) or a podcast-specific platform like Podomatic, which boasts that it has more than 2 million podcasts from around the world; Libsyn, which launched in 2004 and says they had more than 2.6 billion downloads in 2014; PodBean, which says they have more than 130,000 podcasters; or SimpleCast, which promotes its "one-click publishing."

2. **Generate a link to your podcast feed (RSS) and connect accordingly.** After you've chosen a place to host your audio, the site will provide you with a link to your podcast RSS feed, which you will then submit to sites like iTunes or Google Play. This RSS connection is free, but may take a few days to be approved once submitted.

QUICK TIP

All content is generally accepted to be made available on apps like iTunes, but one piece that's important to remember is that if your content is of mature subject matter or has any mature language, it needs to be marked as "explicit."

Chapter 18

PROMOTION STRATEGY

If a podcast is made, but no one listens, does it even exist? Promotion is a key part of your podcasting journey! Here are some common practices that will help promote your podcast once it's ready to be shared.

CREATE A TEASER

This is usually a 1-3 minute piece of audio that serves as the "trailer" for your podcast. It may include some clips from the episodes in the series, or just a voiceover from the host(s) talking about what the show has to offer. It will include information about the release date and where people can find out more. The ultimate goal of the teaser to to get a jump start on subscribers. With the active teaser, people can immediately subscribe and you can start to build an audience before the first episode is even released. One podcast that got extensive hype with just the teaser was *Ear Hustle*, the Radiotopia podcast that was produced from within a prison.

SHARE WITHIN YOUR NETWORK

Like any good marketing strategy, you need to leverage your own personal network (P2P). Share on your social media channels and give the links for any guests or co-hosts to share within their network as well. A creative way to do this is to take advantage of programs like SpareMin, which turns audio files into video files (with an animated audio line that matches the sounds in your podcast). This is more eye-catching and appealing for algorithms on platforms like Twitter and Facebook.

TEAM UP WITH OTHER PODCASTERS

If there is a podcast whose audiences would be interested in hearing about your podcast, reach out! Try to get a spot as a guest on that podcast, or offer to team up for a collaboration and have that host on your podcast. Listeners build strong ties with hosts and will follow where they go. This can also lead to partnership opportunities in the future. It is good to foster these types of relationships.

PROMOTE TO TARGET AUDIENCES

Think about your niche audience and meet them where they're at. If you have a fitness podcast, see if you can team up with a specific gym and get signage/promotion through them. If you are targeting a pre-existing audience for a business, promote the podcast through all methods of communication (direct mail, website, newsletter, etc).

🔍 DID YOU KNOW?

Podcast networks like Gimlet will tap into listeners on their top-rated shows to promote new shows that they plan to release. They typically do this though "bonus" episodes.

Chapter 19

AUDIENCE ENGAGEMENT

Most podcast audiences are eager to stay engaged with podcasts, even after they're done listening. Some shows decide to call out for listeners to send emails, voice notes or texts in order to engage with the show.

Depending on your format and goals, you may want to create social media channels for your podcast so audiences can stay engaged that way. You may also choose to promote your own personal social media channels, especially if you are trying to position yourself as a thought leader and increase your personal following.

Another effective way to engage your audience is through the creation of a website. Most podcasts will feature guests, or being on location and offering additional content (like photos and videos) can be exciting. Audiences can imagine what the host looks like or where they're recording, but seeing what it looks like in reality helps your audience build more of a connection and gives you extra space for additional calls to action.

If you're a business, it's beneficial to have a page on your website dedicated to the podcast, where you can house all the audio embeds, include transcripts (for accessibility and SEO) and hopefully increase your website's traffic and time spent on page.

QUICK TIP

Create social media channels for your podcast to keep your followers engaged even when they're not listening.

Chapter 20

HIRING SUPPORT FOR YOUR PODCAST

If you're having trouble doing it all yourself or you're overseeing the podcast creation for a business, you might want to hire external help. Here are the different positions/roles you might want to consider hiring for.

HOST

Having an engaging host is a very important part of your podcast. Think critically about the voices you include in your podcast. Finding the right role for each of the people you want to include can be tricky, but it's imperative to your podcast's success. The person with the most amount of knowledge in the given subject that you're focusing on does not necessarily need to be the host. Choose someone who is engaging, versatile and does not sound like they're reading off a script all the time.

Many of the journalistic-style podcasts outlined earlier in the book have a script, but the host delivers it in a conversational way. This type of script writing and delivery takes significant time to master and is best left to a professional.

Here are some suggestions for when you may need to hire additional voices:

- Hire a freelance journalist to moderate discussions or provide a voiceover to link certain parts of your podcast

- Hire a voiceover talent to read your ads

- Hire an actor to read your blogs as a dramatic monologue

If you are going to create a first wave style of podcast and you want to conduct conversational interviews as the host, it's best to have some sort of loose plan. Map out talking points in advance and any key message you want to say at the beginning or end, but don't write it out word for word. Have a list with bullet points in front of you as you conduct the interview but allow yourself the flexibility to follow up on points that come up that you may not have been expecting. Don't be afraid to be human: if something is funny, laugh! If your guest mentioned something that you didn't understand, it's likely your audience didn't either, so follow up with a question to clarify.

AUDIO TECHNICIAN

As a beginner, the recording can be done by one person (which is sometimes the same person who is the host and editor). If you're willing to invest in a higher-quality production, it is worth hiring someone as an audio technician/producer to be present while you're recording. Their job would be to ensure the audio quality and content is meeting the agreed upon standards.

For instance, if you want to get a clean, crisp interview recording, the producer would monitor the conversation and note if there were any moments where there may have been a hitch in the recording quality. Something as little as bumping the mic, clapping your hands or speaking slightly off-mic can impact the recording and potentially ruin a key moment in the conversation. Not everything can be fixed in post-production and this would ensure that you have all the necessary assets for your podcast.

EDITOR/SOUND DESIGNER

If you're looking to create a first wave style of podcast, you can edit on your own, or hire a company to "clean up" your audio and add music for a cleaner, slicker sound. It's a fairly inexpensive way to get a more professional sounding podcast. Companies like Podcasting Press, Resonate Recordings and Audio Bag can do it for you, no matter where you're located.

If you're savvy enough to do your own editing, we'll get into what kind of software you can use in the next chapter.

PRODUCER

If you have an idea for a podcast, but you're not sure how to organize the idea, or are having trouble choosing what would be the best format and layout of each episode, then it might be best to hire a producer. This person will hold a consultation session to figure out what you're hoping to accomplish and then be able to give you an outline of your series and each episode. If you're looking to conduct interviews, they may also help pre-screen potential guests and do some scripting for you. Often times producers can also have the ability to edit and/or host.

FULL PRODUCTION AGENCY

If you want creative input, but would rather be hands off with the actual recording and editing of the piece, you would be best to hire an agency to create your podcast. Similar to hiring a video production company, agencies will work with you to capture the content you wish to include, but then handle all of the media management, editing, producing and voiceover. This type of investment is best suited for businesses who wish to invest in their podcast as a method of content marketing. Check out Pacific Content and Gimlet Creative (examples of their work were mentioned in Chapter 6).

I've made podcasts for thought leaders, agencies, private sector businesses and nonprofits. In the next section, I'll give you a look behind the curtain in the creation of two of my recent projects. Get ready to read about the full step-by-step process, including what equipment I used, how I edited the audio and examples of how you can apply the tactics I've outlined throughout this book. This is where you will really get a sense of how it all comes together.

> ### 🔎 DID YOU KNOW?
>
> The most successful conversational podcasts may not be scripted, but still have talking points mapped out in advance. They also often have producers pre-interview guests so they know what kind of conversations will take place on the show.

KEY TAKEAWAYS
Part 4: Doing it Yourself

- Decide on your format/audience before you start
- Invest in the appropriate equipment
- Get to know what apps/software are available to help you accomplish your goals
- Be intentional about your branding
- Take note of what feeds you and what depletes you
- Consider hiring help, accordingly

Part 5

HOW I DID IT

Chapter 21

BEHIND THE SCENES: *A PITCH FOR CHANGE*

"A Pitch for Change is a podcast about what it takes to create a successful business that also has a positive social impact."

That was the opening script I read as the host at the top of every episode of the podcast, so I figured it was the best way to start off this chapter, too!

A Pitch for Change was a branded podcast that I created for the nonprofit organization World Vision Canada. They hold an annual pitch competition with $50,000 up for grabs to fund a local social enterprise. They wanted to do a podcast that would ultimately promote the challenge, position some of their experts as thought leaders in the industry and reach new audiences. Hence the creation of *A Pitch for Change*. In this chapter I'm going to walk you through the steps I took to create this podcast.

A Pitch for Change is a serialized, documentary style podcast that followed a group of young entrepreneurs as they launched a social enterprise. The plan was for me to follow one of the shortlisted teams (called Lumbrick) for three months, leading up to the pitch day. They also wanted to incorporate expert voices throughout the series.

The final product? An eight-episode mini-series, with each episode being about 15 minutes in length. Equipment used to record:

- 1 Zoom H6 recorder
- 3 lavalier mics

ABOVE *a recording session with Lumbrick.*

ABOVE *the Lumbrick team and I after their pitch.*

I conducted all the interviews and recorded the team each week throughout the process. I captured live tape of them working, meeting with their advisors and practising their pitch.

On the actual pitch day, there were a total of five teams presenting to a live audience and three judges. I brought on an extra person to help me record the live tape and reflective interviews throughout the event.

At the end of each recording session, I did media management; I categorized the audio, labeled it with dates, names, and key bullets about what was recorded.

Once all the recording was complete, I brought on a co-producer and editor. In order to form the story, we followed the following steps:

#1 BRAIN DUMP

I told my co-producer everything I knew about the story: highlights that stood out to me, key themes I wanted to highlight and potential gaps I thought we might have.

#2 STORYBOARDING

We came up with a rough outline that incorporated all the major bullets and put the story in order.

#3 CLIP CUTTING

We divided up all the recording sessions and started listening through to pull quotes that aligned with our story outline and anything else that was noteworthy that may have slipped through the cracks.

#4 REVISITING THE STORY OUTLINE WITH CLIPS

Now that we had specific clips we wanted to include in the story, we discussed exactly what order they would go in and outlined scripting notes that coincided with each clip.

#5 WRITE THE SCRIPT

I would write the script and lay out all the clips on a timeline in my editing software (Adobe Audition).

#6 DO A ROUGH READ

We did a rough read and played the clips in the order we had previously determined. We'd then shift clips around, pull additional clips or cut clips as needed.

#7 RECORD

Record the narration and export a rough cut to be shared with a focus group for feedback.

#8 MAKE FINAL EDITS BASED ON FEEDBACK

Once all the episodes had the story locked in, we brought on an audio technician to do levelling. His job was to make sure all the audio sounded as good as it could (ie. minimizing background noise) and then made sure the levels were consistent and underlying music was never too overbearing.

#9 LEVELLING THE AUDIO AND FINAL EXPORT

For this project, I then handed the podcast back to World Vision Canada who were in charge of the marketing, hosting and supplementary website creation.

> ## 🔎 DID YOU KNOW?
>
> For a project like the one outlined in this chapter, it takes about an hour of editing for every minute of audio produced.

Chapter 22

BEHIND THE SCENES: *NEW LENS TRAVEL*

In this chapter I'm going to provide a more detailed look at the editing process for a podcast I created. This was for New Lens Travel: a social enterprise that runs reverse volunteer trips where people learn from local storytellers in countries across Africa.

Before launching a specific podcast series with the business, I created what I call an "audio trailer." This can be used as an introduction for the business in the audio world and can be sent to clients, embedded on their homepage or used as an introduction on podcast platforms to start building an initial audience base.

Below is the transcript of the interview I did with the founder, Jacky Habib. Now, I'm lucky because she was well spoken and had very thorough answers. But this also means there was a lot of editing to do in post-production to get this down to about 2-3 minutes (which is the ideal length for something like this).

After the transcript of the raw audio, I will include the transcript of the edited, final product. You'll be able to see how I pieced together a narrative, just using the subject's answers to my questions.

RAW TRANSCRIPT

AMANDA: *Why did you start New Lens Travel?*

JACKY: *I started New Lens Travel after being inspired when I lived in Ghana. So, a few years ago I worked in Ghana as a media trainer and I connected with a ton of really interesting and creative storytellers, essentially. There were people in media. They were journalists and filmmakers and photographers and people who were brilliant and really talented in what they were doing and they had a local following but not so much of an international following. And I was really intrigued by their work because when we think of Africa and we think of travelling, we often don't think of experiencing that through a local storyteller. And I met all of these brilliant people doing really interesting work and felt like there was an opportunity to connect them with the world. And these* *are people who are using whatever medium that they're in to rewrite narrative about the continent. As we know, Africa has not been represented well historically in media and pop culture and there are still problematic ways that we think about the continent and the way it's covered in news and all of that. So I thought, what better way to go to a place and to find out what's really happening behind the scenes than to engage with essentially these professionals that are storytellers.*

AMANDA: *Talk about some of the mediums that they're using to tell their stories.*

JACKY: *So these people are journalists and a journalist's work looks very diverse. I mean, they could be producing a morning show on a radio station or they could be doing hard-hitting investigative news. Cracking down on people... um... I forget where I was going with this thought...*

AMANDA: *That's ok you can stop and restart.*

JACKY: *Sure. Or they could be doing more hard-hitting investigative type work. There's also people like filmmakers, photographers, bloggers and cartoonists and others who are using media and sometimes art to tell stories about where they're from and share other people's experiences. As a journalist myself, I've always felt really privileged* *to hear other people's stories. When I was living in Ghana, when I was living in Kenya, when I was travelling for work -- I spent my time moving around from place to place talking to people. Having conversations and finding out what they're up to and what's going on and hearing their perspectives and then trying to distil their message to another audience and I felt like that was incredibly valuable and that storytellers are so well connected with other people and they really have good sense of what's going on in a place and I thought to myself, it's not right that when people go to Africa and they want to travel and they want to make a difference in the world, they often end up doing things that really don't make a difference at all and they don't end up connecting with people in the way that storytellers can. And so, I thought, you know, there's an opportunity here to do something.*

AMANDA: *Talk about some of the countries, specifically, that you're working in, in Africa.*

JACKY: *So New Lens Travel works in both Ghana and Kenya. Ghana is a country in west Africa and Kenya is a country in east Africa. They're both very different... on opposite sides of the continent and I have strong ties to both – having lived and worked as a journalist in both countries and so that's how I really developed my own network* *there and connected with these phenomenal storytellers and that's what really drives me in wanting to connect people with them too.*

AMANDA: *Beautiful. So, if you were going to describe what New Lens Travel stands for, what would you say?*

JACKY: *I called it New Lens Travel because I want this experience to be one that really shapes people's perspectives and essentially gives them a new lens... on the world, on people, on creatives, on Africa and there's so much space to really shift our perspectives when it comes to these issues and to really dispel some common beliefs and to unlearn some things that subconsciously, we've picked up from the world: assumptions about other people and other places. So that's why I called it new lens. And I hope that people interacting with New Lens Travel and especially people who come on the trips have such a transformational experience that it really does shift their perspectives in a way that, you know, my travels and my work has changed who I am.*

AMANDA: *And how has it changed who you are?*

JACKY: *I've always been interested in development work and charity and giving back and all of those good things and then I was living in Ghana – I* *had volunteered and I had travelled in a bunch of other countries – but that was one of the first experiences, I would say, that stood out to me in terms of challenging some of my misconceptions and some of the beliefs I held that I didn't even know I had. And so that was really interesting for me. At the same time, I started thinking about the ways we often engage with people in an international context. And when I say we I'm talking about westerns, foreigners people who are not from a country and often try to jump in and help. Very well intentioned but often there isn't such positive outcomes of a short, two-week trip digging a well or doing something like that that a local laborer could do much better and much more cost effective. And so, one of the important things I think that should come out of an international experience is shifted perspectives. And is those relationships because I think it can lead to so much more and really good, tangible outcomes for the future. But I think that having these conversations and learning is one of the best ways to start. And for me that's through storytelling.*

AMANDA: *Beautiful. Now talk about the problem with the current power dynamic when people are typically going overseas...*

JACKY: *Typically, when people go overseas, they're sent as teachers or trainers or mentors in some* *capacity and New Lens Travel is really about flipping that power dynamic so that the power is with the locals, where it should be and instead, us as foreigners, go to learn from locals.*

AMANDA: *Perfect. I think we have a lot here and you're so well spoken too. So now, do you want to slate yourself? You can do a couple.*

JACKY: *Sure. My name is Jacky Habib. I'm a journalist and I'm the founder of New Lens travel... or um... my name is Jacky Habib I'm a social entrepreneur... or... My name is Jacky Habib. I'm a journalist and I'm also a social entrepreneur. I split my time between Canada and a few different places in Africa where I run my company New Lens Travel... um... ya I don't know...*

AMANDA: *I think that's good! Done.*

QUICK TIP

Even though you may be doing a lot of editing in post-production, you still want your interview subject to sound natural. Honour their pacing in order to accurately capture their essence and cadence as a speaker.

Now, you'll notice a lot of my questions were sparked by things she was saying. I don't like pre-scripting questions before going into situations like this.

Also important to note, this interview took about 12 minutes and the final product is about two minutes. Here it is.

TRANSCRIPT OF FINAL PIECE

JACKY: *As a journalist myself, I've always felt really privileged to hear other people's stories. When I was living in Ghana, when I was living in Kenya, when I was travelling for work -- I spent my time moving around from place to place talking to people. Having conversations and finding out what they're up to and what's going on and hearing their perspectives... and I met all of these brilliant people doing really interesting work and felt like there was an opportunity to connect them with the world. And these are people who are using whatever medium that they're in to rewrite narrative about the continent.*

Africa has not been represented well historically in media and pop culture and there are still problematic ways that we think about the continent and so I thought, what better way to go to a place and to find out what's really happening behind the scenes than to engage with filmmakers, photographers, bloggers and cartoonists and others who are using media and sometimes art to tell stories about where they're from and share other people's experiences.

At the same time, I started thinking about the ways we often engage with people in an international context. And when I say we I'm talking about westerns, foreigners people who are not from a country and often try to jump in and help.

New Lens Travel is really about flipping that power dynamic so that the power is with the locals, where it should be. And so, one of the important things I think that should come out of an international experience is shifted perspectives and essentially a new lens... on the world, on people, on creatives, on Africa.

I hope that people interacting with New Lens Travel and especially people who come on the trips have such a transformational experience that it really does shift their perspectives in a way that, you know, my travels and my work has changed who I am.

My name is Jacky Habib and I'm the founder of New Lens Travel.

You'll notice I've pieced together sentences (and even edited out words here and there) in order to make the narrative flow. With my background in journalism, I'm always mindful to keep the intention and message of the sentence the same. I'm not constructing new thoughts, but rather putting together a story. I also made sure to take out anything that became repetitive and only use the best, most concise clips.

For instance, she spoke a lot about the power dynamic that typically occurs when people travel overseas to try and help. In the interview, she originally explained it like this:

> *"I started thinking about the ways we often engage with people in an international content. And when I say we I'm talking about westerns, foreigners people who are not from a country and often try to jump in and help. Very well intentioned but often there isn't such positive outcomes of a short, two-week trip digging a well or doing something like that that a local laborer could do much better and much more cost effective. And so, one of the important things I think that should come out of an international experience is shifted perspectives. And is those relationships because I think it can lead to so much more and really good, tangible outcomes for the future."*

The most concise way she explained it, though, was after I specifically asked her about the power dynamic.

> *"Typically, when people go overseas, they're sent as teachers or trainers or mentors in some capacity and New Lens Travel is really about flipping that power dynamic so that the power is with the locals, where it should be and instead, us as foreigners, go to learn from locals."*

I then took the best of both answers and edited it together in order to get the idea across in the most clear, concise and powerful way.

> *"I started thinking about the ways we often engage with people in an international content. And when I say we I'm talking about westerns, foreigners people who are not from a country and often try to jump in and help."*

+

> *"New Lens Travel is really about flipping that power dynamic so that the power is with the locals, where it should be."*

This is the type of editing that can be extremely time consuming if you are new to it, but it's also some of the most rewarding part of the process if you enjoy building narratives, like I do. I live for this stuff!

When I'm making these kinds of edits, I'm also very intentional about the way it ends. It should leave you *feeling* something. The last clip has to be powerful and the music has to match. You'll know when it's right. It gives you the shivers! In Jacky's case, I know I nailed it.

> *"I hope that people interacting with New Lens Travel and especially people who come on the trips have such a transformational experience that it really does shift their perspectives in a way that, you know, my travels and my work has changed who I am. My name is Jacky Habib and I'm the founder of New Lens Travel."*

So good!

You may have noticed I slightly edited her slate, where she says her name and title. When we recorded it she did two versions. I opted for the shorter one and proceeded to make it even shorter by removing the part where she also called herself a journalist. Of course, I did this with her permission.

The reasoning?

The shorter slate left for a more powerful ending to the piece. The edit also did not alter the way Jacky wanted to present herself, since the piece opens with her talking about her work as a journalist. In these situations I will sometimes even export two different versions of the edit so the client I'm working with can hear the difference. It's attention to small details like this that can really set the tone for the piece as a whole.

KEY TAKEAWAYS
Part 5: How I Did It

- When working on a more complex podcast topic, doing a "brain dump" can help you sort your thoughts and determine your direction
- Taking notes during recording sessions will help you with editing later
- Involve others in your review process. Get feedback before going live.
- Slickly produced podcasts take a lot of time but it's worth it!
- It's always best to record more than you think you need and then edit it down to include the best parts

CONCLUSION

And there you have it!

In case you finished this whole book and you're thinking "wait, I forgot everything I just read!", here are the three major highlights...

1. Podcasts are having their moment. There are lots of listeners, appetite from advertisers and yes, a lot of content that's already out there. But that doesn't mean you should shy away from making your own.

2. If you are going to make your own podcast, put some thought into the format, genre, equipment and target audience.

3. The podcasting landscape is only going to expand. Get ready for more branded podcasts, podcast celebrities to emerge and for more live events.

But if I can leave you with one last notion, I would like it to be a reminder to have fun! I've had numerous consultations with people who want to give it a shot but feel overwhelmed and nervous. Just remember that in reality, there is a lot of flexibility with podcasts. There are no specific parameters for how long each episode has to be or how many people should be involved. It's totally up to you. Give it a try and don't be too hard on yourself. Especially if you read this book, I know you're going to be great.

"*Words mean more than what is set down on paper. It takes the human voice to infuse them with shades of a deeper meaning.*"

—MAYA ANGELOU

GLOSSARY

CALL TO ACTION: which may also be called a CTA. This is the action you would like for the audience to take after engaging with a piece of content. In a podcast context, this is referring to any asks made of the audience, usually at the end of the podcast (ie. to subscribe on iTunes or check out the website).

CHAT CAST: Probably the most frequently heard. This is where two co-hosts will talk about a range of topics, in a conversational style. They may incorporate audio if it relates to the given topic they're discussing or have on guests to be interviewed.

CPM: cost per mille (or thousand), which is referring to the base cost you would charge for an ad, which would increase for every 1000 listeners of your podcast.

DRIVING MUSIC: This is music that is typically used in transitions or under a script of a podcast. It helps sets the tone and feeling of a particular moment. If done well, the audience does not really notice it's there. Its main purpose is to move the podcast along.

EVERGREEN: This is a genre of podcast that outlines information or a story that is not time sensitive. You can listen to this at any time and find the content presented relevant.

IDENTIFYING MUSIC: This is the music that defines your podcast. It's typically used just at the beginning and end of each episode and the audience will come to associate it with your podcast/brand. It should align with the overall mood of the podcast.

LIVE TAPE: This is when you are recording something that is happening live, in real time. When you incorporate it in a podcast, it gives listeners the sense that they are "there" at the event.

MID-ROLL: An ad that runs in the middle of an episode of a podcast.

MINI-SERIES: This typically includes about 6-10 episodes in total. This collection of episodes can either be serialized (which requires listeners to consume in order), or have each episode standing on its own, but in either case, are linked by an overarching theme.

ONE PERSON SHOW: This is tough to pull off, but is typically done by comedians (who will essentially just do a standup act) or it will be done with a pre-written script with information someone wants to share.

PRE-ROLL: An ad that runs at the beginning of an episode of a podcast.

RAW AUDIO: Unedited audio that you've recorded. This can either be of an interview or of ambient sound.

REFLECTIVE TAPE: An interview with someone who is recalling on past occurences. This is the opposite of "live" tape.

SERIALIZED: This is a podcast done in a journalistic style, where a story is told episode-by-episode. You will likely need to listen to the episodes in the order they are released. Each episode will highlight some sort of pivot in the story. All the episodes, together, will tell the story.

SLATE: This is a term used in TV, radio and podcasting, where you will get a subject to say their name and title while recording, which will make it easier to attribute clips in the editing process. Sometimes people will also incorporate this into the finished product, especially when doing a documentary-style piece.

SOUND UP: This is an editing tactic used when you want listeners to pay attention to a specific piece of audio. In most cases the audio is already underlying and then there is a moment where a specific part is highlighted by bringing the sound up in the edit. The narration will also stop so the sound up can be heard clearly. This can sometimes be just a background sound (ie. there is ambient sound of a street and then the sound of a car horn honking is brought louder) or it can be something a subject says (ie. a long speech is droning very low in the background but then a certain sentence is made louder so it can be noted).

TEASER: This is similar to a movie trailer, but for a podcast series. It's used to give audiences a taste of what's included in an upcoming podcast series. These are usually under 5 minutes in length and incorporate music, clips from a few of the episodes and/or the host(s) talking.

THEMATIC SERIES: This is a podcast that covers a certain theme of content throughout a series. Episodes are standalone stories and can be listened to in any order. This is similar to current affairs programming that we're familiar with on TV. Themes are usually broad topics, like entrepreneurship, personal finance or matters of the heart.

VIGNETTES: These are short stories, rants or tips that can be grouped into an ongoing series or a mini-series. They are typically about 3-5 minutes long and highlight quick bites of information.

VO: Voice over, usually scripted, recorded and edited into the podcast in post-production. This is done by the host and provides a narrative for the podcast.

```
 PPS
 ___
 PUB
```

We believe that there is no better way to expand your knowledge than with a good book, which is why we focus on publishing works that empower readers to succeed in the modern world. From business, to relationships, to health & wellness, our passion is finding fresh authors who have invaluable insights and are eager to share them with you.

At PPS Publishing, we are proud to publish works from thought leaders who are trailblazers in their fields. As a team of book-loving women, we are especially committed to publishing women authors and allies.

For more great reads, visit our website or connect with us on social media.

@ppspublishing   @ppspublishing

PPSPUBLISHING.COM